Managing the Customer Experience

Also available from ASQ Quality Press:

Linking Customer and Employee Satisfaction to the Bottom Line
Derek Allen and Morris Wilburn

Competing for Customers and Winning with Value:
Breakthrough Strategies for Market Dominance
R. Eric Reidenbach and Reginald W. Goeke

Analysis of Customer Satisfaction Data
Derek Allen and Tanniru R. Rao

Measuring Customer Satisfaction: Survey Design, Use, and Statistical
Analysis Methods, Second Edition
Bob E. Hayes

Measuring and Managing Customer Satisfaction: Going for the Gold
Sheila Kessler

ANSI/ISO/ASQ Q10002-2004: Quality management—Customer
satisfaction—Guidelines for complaints handling in organizations
ANSI/ISO/ASQ

The Certified Manager of Quality/Organizational Excellence Handbook,
Third Edition
Russell T. Westcott, editor

The Quality Toolbox, Second Edition
Nancy R. Tague

Making Change Work: Practical Tools for Overcoming Human Resistance
to Change
Brien Palmer

Business Performance through Lean Six Sigma: Linking the Knowledge
Worker, the Twelve Pillars, and Baldrige
James T. Schutta

To request a complimentary catalog of ASQ Quality Press publications,
call 800-248-1946, or visit our Web site at http://qualitypress.asq.org.

Managing the Customer Experience

A Measurement-Based Approach

Morris Wilburn

ASQ Quality Press
Milwaukee, Wisconsin

American Society for Quality, Quality Press, Milwaukee 53203
© 2007 by American Society for Quality
All rights reserved. Published 2006
Printed in the United States of America
12 11 10 09 08 07 06   5 4 3 2 1

Library of Congress Cataloging-in-Publication Data

Wilburn, Morris, 1953–
   Managing the customer experience : a measurement-based approach / Morris
Wilburn.
     p. cm.
   ISBN-13: 978-0-87389-702-0 (pbk. : alk. paper)
   1. Consumer satisfaction.   2. Customer relations.   3. Customer services.
I. Title.

   HF5415.335.W55   2006
   658.'12—dc22

                                                2006024190

Publisher: William A. Tony
Acquisitions Editor: Matt Meinholz
Project Editor: Paul O'Mara
Production Administrator: Randall Benson

ASQ Mission: The American Society for Quality advances individual, organizational, and community excellence worldwide through learning, quality improvement, and knowledge exchange.

Attention Bookstores, Wholesalers, Schools, and Corporations: ASQ Quality
Press books, videotapes, audiotapes, and software are available at quantity
discounts with bulk purchases for business, educational, or instructional use. For
information, please contact ASQ Quality Press at 800-248-1946, or write to ASQ
Quality Press, P.O. Box 3005, Milwaukee, WI 53201-3005.

To place orders or to request a free copy of the ASQ Quality Press Publications
Catalog, including ASQ membership information, call 800-248-1946. Visit our
Web site at www.asq.org or http://qualitypress.asq.org.

Quality Press
600 N. Plankinton Avenue
Milwaukee, Wisconsin 53203
Call toll free 800-248-1946
Fax 414-272-1734
www.asq.org
http://qualitypress.asq.org
http://standardsgroup.asq.org
E-mail: authors@asq.org

♾ Printed on acid-free paper

*To my parents, who worked hard and sacrificed much so
that I would have an easier life than they had.*

Contents

List of Figures and Tables

Preface

At the time I began planning this book, there already were good books on the collection of customer satisfaction and loyalty data. They addressed the writing of questions for use in questionnaires, principles of questionnaire design, different modes of administering the questionnaire along with their respective advantages and disadvantages, generic lists of product and service attributes, and so on.

The topic of analytical techniques also seemed to be well covered. Marketing researchers had already written applied books on advanced analytical techniques that covered the waterfront—multiple regression, logistic regression, discriminant analysis, canonical correlation, factor analysis, structural equation models, multidimensional scaling (MDS), and so on. Extensive treatments on individual techniques were also available, with some books exceeding a thousand pages in length.

In spite of this and what was learned from practical experience, the customer loyalty research programs of most companies fell short of their intended purpose. Some of the reasons for failure had to do with the conceptual framework of the drivers of loyalty. Specifically, most customer loyalty programs do a poor job of addressing the emotional aspect of the service experience and its influence on customer loyalty.

In addition, brand image is usually not addressed as well as it could be. This is partly attributable to the traditional belief that brand and brand image are tools for acquiring customers, not retaining or getting them to spend more. But the fact is that brand and brand image often influence customer loyalty.

Much of Chapter 1 is devoted to these two issues.

There is also a lack of recognition that customer loyalty management requires multiple research studies that have different objectives and methods and are designed to form an integrated research program. Chapter 2 discusses the objectives of a customer loyalty research program and describes the individual studies in that program. Subsequent chapters illustrate how those studies complement each other.

Another area of weakness involves analyzing the data in a manner that enables the research sponsor to make management decisions. One of the complaints most often voiced by loyalty research sponsors is that they can't use the results of the research. Chapter 3 is devoted to analyzing the data in a manner that enables the research sponsor to make management decisions—in particular, the construction of what in management circles have traditionally been called decision tools.

Chapter 4 continues this discussion and also discusses the challenges that arise in constructing these tools.

By design, most of this book is written at a fairly high conceptual level because, as noted earlier, there are other books on how to collect the needed data and how to use the analytical techniques implied by the decision tool discussions. An exception is part of Chapter 4, which alerts the reader to certain important analytical issues not addressed in existing books.

Morris Wilburn

Acknowledgments

Over the course of my career I have been privileged to work with a number of very good researchers and consultants at several companies—Market Probe, The Gallup Organization, SDR Consulting, and Bardsley and Neidhart. A substantial portion of whatever knowledge or insight is evidenced in this book came out of that experience.

This book would not have been possible without the support of my current company, Market Probe. In addition, Bob White and Heather Nagel performed invaluable proofreading tasks, and Latoya Ellis and Bonnie Lockwood produced the graphics. Allen Vivian, Tom Fusso, Leopold Zuniga, Richard Lichvar, Eva Lau, Shaun Hill, Bruce Fritzges, and ASQ reviewers David P. Crowell, Garry Schultz, and Daniel Zrymiak provided very valuable comments and suggestions.

I would also like to express my gratitude to ASQ Quality Press: Annemieke Hytinen, former ASQ Quality Press acquisitions editor; and Paul D. O'Mara, ASQ Quality Press project editor.

1

The Customer Experience

This chapter argues that programs to manage customer loyalty often overlook important aspects of the customer's experience with the company. These aspects are as follows:

- Brand image

- Customer emotions evoked by contact with service employees

- The shopping environment

These aspects and how they interrelate are discussed in this chapter. The subject of relationship is also discussed, as well as empathy shown by employees toward customers.

INTRODUCTION

One of the fundamental changes in business in America over the past three decades has been a shift away from trying to acquire *as many customers* as possible toward retaining and then obtaining as much business as possible from *each customer*.

One reason for this change is that many product categories are no longer growing in terms of the number of people in the category. This is because most American households already have, for example, an automobile, a TV, a washing machine, and so on.

Another reason is the greatly increased competition from both domestic and foreign sources. In many product categories, there are a half dozen or so substantial competitors, each offering multiple models of high-quality products and covering a wide range in terms of price and features. For example, a person seeking to purchase a home audio receiver will usually find several stores within a 45-minute drive, with each store having four or five brands and each brand having multiple models. Even more brands and models are available on the Internet.

Related to this, in an effort to reduce the number of competitors and better meet the needs of their customers, many companies are focusing only on certain consumer segments. This change has had the effect of reducing the potential size of the company's customer base.

Another reason is that research studies that focus on the lifetime value of a behaviorally loyal customer have produced very impressive results in a number of product/service categories, and these results have been reported in the business press.

Because of this, many companies have established survey-research-based customer loyalty programs. However, over the past few years there has been an increased awareness, especially in service-oriented businesses, that these programs do not address all of the company's actions that influence repurchase behavior. Consequently, efforts have been made to identify and understand the actions that have been overlooked.

Many of those efforts have focused on brand and on aspects of consumer motivation that are emotional in nature. Some have focused on what they call "the customer experience" with the brand or company. Some of the more prominent writings are Schmitt (2003), Schmitt (1999), Smith and Wheeler (2002), Shaw and Ivens (2002), Pine and Gilmore (1999), and Gilmore and Pine (2002).

I have some fundamental differences with these writings, but I believe that thinking in terms of the customer's experience with the company has certain benefits, hence the title of this book. One benefit is that the term "the company" encompasses all of the customer's contacts with the company. Another benefit is that the term "customer experience" implies a customer-centric perspective. Related to this, the term "experience" implies a focus on more than the functional aspects of the company's service and products.

This chapter represents my attempt to identify the aspects of the customer experience that are not addressed in the loyalty programs of most companies. The chapter ends with a comprehensive picture of the customer experience—comprehensive in that it includes the aspects that traditionally have been included and those that have not—conceptualized in a way that enables a company to manage that experience.

THE EFFECT OF BRAND IMAGE ON THE CUSTOMER'S EXPERIENCE

To paraphrase a definition by Aaker (1991), a *brand* is a name, term, or symbol intended to identify the products or services of the seller and to differentiate them from those of competitors. Brands can be many things, including the name of the manufacturer or retailer (for example, Sony or

Burger King), references to important product benefits (for example, Easy-Off Oven Cleaner), or names invented to sound attractive (modern, scientific, or sophisticated, such as Accenture, Textronics, and Lexus, respectively).

The definition of brand provided earlier contains the phrase "differentiate them from those of competitors." More is meant by "differentiation" than simply preventing shoppers from mistaking the product of one company for that of another. A brand also gives the consumer a reason to buy one product instead of another. It does this by adding something intangible to the purchase, ownership, or use of the product. That "something" may be perceptions about broad functional benefits of the product, such as overall quality, or it may be emotional benefits (for example, security, increased status, or meeting the need to nurture).

These benefits are conveyed by *brand image*. Brand image has traditionally been thought of as a method for acquiring customers, but it also influences current customers. Consider the following:

- An image of overall quality will make an owner more satisfied with a product. This effect is even greater if the product is such that its quality cannot be fully evaluated, even by the user. Home heating equipment is one example of this.

- If a food brand has an image of being healthful, the satisfaction of health-conscious consumers will be increased.

- In some product categories, if a product has an image of being for a certain type of person (for example, sophisticated or successful people), customers who want to be members of that group will increase their self-esteem by owning that brand.

- If a restaurant has an image of being family oriented, the satisfaction of some patrons will be increased.

- In business markets, purchase of a name brand provides the emotional benefit of security, as illustrated by the advertising statement, "No one ever got fired for buying IBM."

- In business markets, an image of being technologically advanced is important for industries in which the pace of technological change is rapid.

Brand/company image adds something intangible to purchasing, owning, or using a product. That "something" may be perceptions about broad functional benefits of the product, such as overall quality, or it may be emotional benefits (for example, security, increased status, or meeting the need to nurture).

Traditionally, companies in most product categories have relied primarily on advertising to establish brand images. In the case of an emotional benefit, a common strategy is to have advertisements consistently depict a certain type of person (for example, a financially successful person) enjoying a commensurate lifestyle and using the brand. Because of those advertisements, a person who wants to be a member of this group (financially successful people, in this example) will mentally associate the brand with the group, and owning or using a product of that brand will increase his or her self-esteem.

The automotive industry can be used to illustrate the establishment of a broad functional benefit. A common practice is for the company's advertisements to consistently depict its vehicles accomplishing difficult tasks under brutal conditions, causing viewers to mentally associate that brand with reliability, thereby establishing a brand image of reliability.

Note that my perspective on brand image is much broader than that of the customer experience writings cited earlier; those writings focus almost entirely on the emotional benefits of a brand, giving little attention to brand-related perceptions about the product's functional benefits. The latter are important; they are often very important in business-to-business industries.

A company decides which images it *should* associate with its brand on the basis of a *brand positioning study*. Formally stated, the purpose of a brand positioning study is to identify a distinct and valued place in the consumer's mind that is not currently occupied by a brand. After this place and the brand images defining it have been identified, the company designs its advertising to convey those images, and it designs new products or modifies existing ones so that they are consistent with those images.

Readers who wish to learn more about brand and brand image should consult Keller (1998) and Aaker (1991 and 1996).

Forces Influencing Brand Image

It was stated earlier that companies in most product categories have traditionally relied primarily on advertising to establish brand images. Brand image is also influenced by the person's experiences with the brand's products, the shopping and purchase experience, product evaluations by objective sources (for example, *Consumer Reports*), word of mouth, opinion leaders, and other sources.

The reader might be surprised by how far some of these forces can reach. For example, among some consumer populations, satisfaction with the service department of a car dealership influences the purchase of brands of cars sold by that dealership. That is quite a reach.

Events beyond the company's control sometimes influence the image of the brand or of one of its products in a way similar to that of marketing communications. For example, the appearance of the Smith & Wesson .44 Magnum pistol in the movie *Dirty Harry* attached strong images to that firearm.

EMOTIONS PRODUCED BY INTERACTIONS WITH SERVICE PERSONNEL

Historically, customer loyalty programs have focused mainly on functional characteristics of the product or service under study (for example, reliability and responsiveness in the case of services). This is why customer loyalty research studies in service categories often have "service quality" in their names, as the word "quality" has a connotation of functionality and objectivity.

This focus flies in the face of decades of psychological research that has found that *behavior is strongly influenced not only by rational calculation but by feelings as well.* Furthermore, a number of studies have found this to be true for consumer behavior.

Managers of loyalty management programs should have more insight into this than they do, even if they have never heard of consumer behavior research. For many years, employees with direct customer contact have known that one of the surest ways to lose a customer is to make him or her appear "wrong," especially if the customer's spouse or friends are present. This also holds true for being disrespectful to the customer, and it may even initiate a heated confrontation.

Barsky and Nash identified certain emotions in the hotel industry by customer segment (Table 1.1).

These findings make intuitive sense. For example, in the luxury segment, the relevant feelings are feeling pampered, relaxed, and sophisticated. In the economy segment, the relevant feelings are feeling comfortable and welcome and being practical.

Feeling comfortable and feeling welcome are relevant in most of the segments. A few words of clarification are needed here regarding feeling "comfortable." Customers were referring to more than physical comfort (for example, a comfortable bed); they also meant that the staff was friendly, attentive, and enthusiastic and could be trusted with messages and wake-up calls. There were also issues pertaining to the arrival of the guest: addressing the guest by name, using courteous and respectful words, and greeting the guest warmly.

Table 1.1   Emotions in the hotel industry by customer segment.

	Economy	Mid-price	Upper Midprice	Upscale	Luxury	Extended Stay	Casino	Upscale Casino
Comfortable	✓	✓	✓	✓		✓		
Welcome	✓	✓	✓	✓		✓		
Content							✓	✓
Pampered					✓			✓
Relaxed					✓			✓
Secure		✓	✓					
Entertained							✓	
Important				✓				
Inspired							✓	
Practical	✓							
Respected						✓		
Sophisticated					✓			
Elegant								
Excited								
Extravagant								
Hip or cool								

Source: J. Barsky and L. Nash, "Customer Satisfaction: Applying Concepts to Industry-wide Measures," *Cornell Hotel and Restaurant Administration Quarterly* 44, no. 5–6 (2003): 177.

By "secure," customers meant that the staff confirmed that persons entering the hotel were indeed guests, staff members were present throughout the hotel, guests needed keys to enter elevators, and the hotel was equipped with security cameras, lighting in interior public areas, and parking lot lighting that could be seen from the guest's room. The door to the guest's room was also an issue, with guests preferring big, sturdy doors.

Edwardson (1998) conducted a study focusing largely on restaurants, miscellaneous retail, clothing retail, and banks. This study identified 220 emotions; those that were found most often are shown in Figure 1.1.

Edwardson also classified emotions by the product category in which they were most often found. This classification is found in Table 1.2.

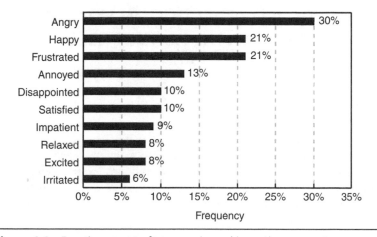

Figure 1.1   Emotions most often experienced in service encounters.

Source: M. Edwardson, "Measuring Consumer Emotions in Service Encounters: An Exploratory Analysis," *Australasian Journal of Market Research* 6, no. 2 (1998): 10.

Table 1.2   Emotions by product category.

Retail Clothing	Anticipation
Relieved	Content
*Grateful	*Relaxed
Happy	Embarrassed
Satisfied	Impatient
Excited	Angry
Content	Annoyed
Indignant	Frustrated
Impatient	*Disappointed
Embarrassed	**Banking**
Annoyed	Surprised
Angry	*Trusting
*Irritated	Encouraged
Frustrated	Curious
Disappointed	Happy
Hospitality	Anxious
Welcome	Nervous
Excited	Angry
Warm	Frustrated
Happy	*Powerless

*Indicates key emotion.

Source: M. Edwardson, "Measuring Consumer Emotions in Service Encounters: An Exploratory Analysis," *Australasian Journal of Market Research* 6, no. 2 (1998): 13.

ANOTHER PERSPECTIVE ON EMOTION: FUNDAMENTAL HUMAN NEEDS

In many instances—but not all—survey research methodology is ill-suited for measuring the intensity of specific emotions; this is best done in one-on-one situations in which the researcher does something like show the respondent pictures or videos of customers in the service experience and then ask the respondent what he or she thinks the customer is feeling.

But there is a way to get around this methodological limitation. Schneider and Bowen (1999) point out that emotions are functions of fundamental human needs, and they show how survey research can be used to measure how well a company meets those needs, thereby indirectly measuring customer emotions.

Over the years, several consumer motivation researchers have developed lists of fundamental human needs that can conceivably be met by products or services. I have consolidated several of those lists, and my own, yielding the list in Table 1.3.

Empirical research suggests that certain needs are found in many consumer service-oriented industries; those needs are security, self-esteem, and justice (including fairness), and they are discussed in this section. Additional needs should be included in your customer loyalty programs on the basis of research in your product category.

Let's begin with self-esteem. A specific example is as follows. A store had a policy that if a customer returned a music CD, saying that the CD was

Table 1.3   Fundamental human needs (listed in alphabetical order).

Acceptance by relevant others	Reward for effort or sacrifice
Autonomy	Security
Cognitive stimulation	Self-esteem
Individuality	Self-expression
Justice (including fairness)	Self-fulfillment
Love	Self-respect
Mastery over environment	Sense of accomplishment
Moral purity	Sense of belonging
Need for cognition (need to understand our environment)	Social acceptance
Need to nurture	Status
Personal growth	Warm relationships with others
Respect	

Source: J. Sheth, B. Mittal, and B. Newman, *Customer Behavior: Consumer Behavior and Beyond* (Fort Worth, TX: Harcourt Brace College Publishers, 1999), 350–351, 363.

defective, the clerk would try to play it on a CD player in the store. If the CD did not play there, the customer would be given a replacement; if it did play, the clerk would tell the customer that nothing was wrong with the CD. The unspoken message of the latter response to the customer was that she did not know how to operate her own audio equipment, or that something was wrong with her equipment. This will probably decrease her self-esteem and therefore her loyalty.

A more common example is a purchase process that makes the customer feel ignorant or unintelligent—for example, using signage or answering customer questions with company jargon.

On the other hand, anything that makes customers believe that a company values their business may increase (or reinforce) their self-esteem and loyalty.

Regarding security, an obvious manifestation is the desire for physical safety (for example, safety while using ATMs). Another is protection from nonviolent crime (for example, identity theft or obtaining the customer's credit card number).

Another manifestation, frequently exhibited, is the general desire for things to happen as the customer expects them to. This desire exists even in affairs of little importance, albeit less strongly. Consequently, if anything causes the customer to doubt the service person's ability or motivation to do his or her job, the outcome of the service experience is brought into doubt in the customer's mind, possibly decreasing the person's loyalty. This effect may occur even if the service turns out to be correct and timely.

There is a variation of this, as follows. In some product categories—housing renovation and automobile servicing, for example—the answers to certain important customer questions, such as cost and length of time required to perform the work, are not known at the beginning because they depend on what the service people find in the course of doing the work. An example in housing renovation is that the company does not know beforehand the degree of insect damage to the existing woodwork.

This is an issue because this uncertainty makes the customer feel less in control and therefore less secure. In such service categories, customer security can be increased by periodic communications from the company on how things are going.

In the case of justice, there are two aspects. One is for oneself to be treated justly; the other is for other people to be treated justly. Some examples of offending behaviors are a company's raising prices during a short-term decrease in availability (for example, gasoline suppliers), not honoring stated product return policies as the customer understands them, or exploiting its workers in sweat shops.

An offending behavior may be more subtle. Americans are accustomed to customer reward programs in certain industries, such as frequent-flier miles in the airline industry and customer membership programs of super-markets. These programs usually do not cause a problem. However, if the programs are administered without tact, some customers will feel as though they are being punished or that the company does not value their patronage. This reaction is more likely to occur when there is another service problem.

The degree to which a company's service meets these needs can be measured in a customer survey by asking the respondent if he or she agrees or disagrees with statements such as the following:

Security—the service representative took the time to determine which products would meet my individual needs

Self-esteem—the service representative made me feel like a valued customer

Justice—the service representative resolved the problem fairly

The specific questions are based on the product category under study.

> When in a service situation, a customer is still a person, having fundamental human needs that influence his or her emotions, which in turn influence his or her repurchase behavior.

ANOTHER ROLE OF SECURITY

Security is more than a fundamental human need. Security is closely related to *trust*. This is an issue because trust is a necessary condition for customer loyalty.

To paraphrase Sheth, Mittal, and Newman (1999), trust has the following elements:

- The customer with trust has sufficient confidence in the company to act or rely on the company

- The company that is trusted is perceived to have three characteristics:

  - The ability to carry out its obligations

  - The willingness to fulfill its obligations

  - The desire to look after not only its own interests, but the customer's as well

The company should consider the impact of trust in everything it does, because there can be no loyalty without trust.

EMPATHY

As is the case in other human endeavors, we sometimes overlook the obvious. One such instance here is that service employees who have direct contact with customers should empathize with customers. This is especially true of service channels or customer contact points designed to resolve customer complaints. In the context under discussion, empathy has the following ingredients:

- Being friendly

- Being aware of the customer's feelings

- Caring about the customer's feelings

- Caring about the customer and meeting his or her needs

- Affirming that the customer's concern or feeling is valid, in the case of problem resolution

- Owning the problem

This is very different from the common practice of dealing with customers in the same way that a farmworker manages the movement of cattle. How can the company get its employees to have (and show) empathy? One method is to show employees videos of service experiences (actual or mock) in which empathy is and is not expressed. A video, as opposed to a written description, is needed because a substantial portion of communication (by both employees and customers) is nonverbal: eye contact, tone of voice, facial expressions, and body language.

Notice that this has implications in the hiring process. While it is true that some employees can be trained to exhibit more empathy than they actually have, this is possible only up to a degree, and even that effect may be temporary. Consequently, the company needs to hire people who are predisposed to empathizing with customers. This reminds us of the saying, "No type or amount of training can get a cat to bark; if you want barking, get a dog."

Readers interested in learning more about empathy can consult Barlow and Maul (2000) and Shaw and Ivens (2002).

The Golden Rule: Do unto others as you would have them do unto you.

THE SHOPPING ENVIRONMENT

The term "shopping environment" is broadly defined here to include everything about the shopping environment except the employees who have direct contact with customers. The latter is addressed in this book as a separate topic.

It is widely known among manufacturers of consumer packaged goods that the aesthetics of the package in which the product is sold influences purchase behavior, and in the case of food, the package sometimes influences the taste of the food. This was determined by experiments as early as the 1930s. It should come as no surprise to us that the shopping environment influences purchase behavior.

Furthermore, there is a need for consistency across a customer's contacts with a company. For example, one car rental company found that customers perceived its cars to be cleaner when the rental facility interior was cleaner (Carbone 2004). The psychological process at work is *generalization*. That is, if customers perceive a characteristic or condition (good or bad) in one part of the company, they tend to perceive that other parts of the company have that same characteristic or condition. This occurs in any given company countless times every day.

To a large extent—but not completely—the issues that we must consider in getting customers to continue purchasing a given product or service are the same ones we must consider in getting consumers to make an initial purchase.

An entire book could be written on this subject. There are consulting companies that do nothing but advise companies on how to design and make their stores more customer friendly; some of them are even specialized, focusing on aesthetics. Consequently, only an overview of this subject will be presented here.

A general issue is that *the customer's shopping experience should be a positive one, irrespective of brand image or other issues.* This is a function of the design and condition (cleanliness, state of repair) of the store, aesthetics, operating processes, breadth of product offerings, brands carried, and other forces.

In many product categories, it is important that the shopping environment be interesting to shoppers. This is especially important among certain customer populations.

There are literally dozens of specific issues about which a company should be concerned, such as the following:

- Congestion inside the store.

- Waiting time. The length of waiting time as perceived by customers can be reduced by anything that diverts the customer's attention from the act of waiting, such as watching television.

- Elderly customers' fear of being jostled by other customers, causing them to lose their balance and fall. This is but one of many issues that will become more relevant as the population ages.

- Arrangement of merchandise. As noted by Underhill (1999), some shoppers, especially women, are uncomfortable bending over a waist-high (or lower) table for very long. This is because of their concern over the social awkwardness that would result from being inadvertently brushed in the buttocks by another customer. Another reason is their concern about attracting unwanted attention of an erotic nature.

- Cleanliness of store. In some cases, a store whose exterior is dirty is perceived by customers as being more likely to have violent crimes committed in the store parking lot.

- The smell of automotive supplies (for example, motor oil) in the fruit section of a supermarket.

A related but distinct issue is mood. The shopping environment can evoke moods. Moods may be very general—that is, either positive or negative—or specific. Consider the different specific moods that would be evoked by the following songs being played over the store's sound system:

The gospel classic "Oh What a Savior!"

The romantic "The First Time Ever I Saw Your Face," by Roberta Flack

The sports anthem "We Will Rock You," by Queen

The soothing "Only Time," by Enya

The lighthearted "All I Wanna Do," by Sheryl Crow

The somber string orchestra piece "Adagio for Strings," by Samuel Barber (used in the movie *Platoon*)

Even the speed of the music can, in some circumstances, influence the amount of time that a customer spends in the store.

Color can also evoke certain specific moods; for example, in some product categories, certain colors can either stimulate or elicit calm.

Some obvious examples pertain to smell—for example, the smell of perfume in the clothing department of a store.

Another issue is that as noted earlier, *the shopping environment should communicate the brand images the company wants to communicate.* This is important for several reasons. One is that advertising will be more effective if it is reinforced by something else (for example, the shopping environment).

But the main reason is that if the shopping environment communicates the same brand images as those of the company's advertising, the functional or emotional benefits provided by those brand images will be experienced by shopping in the store. This is important, extremely so in some product categories.

How can the shopping environment communicate brand image? One way to think about this is that the shopping environment should have the look and feel of the brand image. How this is accomplished depends somewhat on the product category and brand image. For example, in a retail clothing situation, an image of "being for affluent people" can be communicated by displaying products in smaller quantities (thereby suggesting a higher price), placing purchases in a fancy shopping bag at checkout, using higher-quality materials in displays and furniture, and having employees dress better than employees in most stores.

Some other examples are as follows:

- McDonald's outlets have play areas for children and pictures of Ronald McDonald to support the brand images of "fun" and "for families"

- The uniforms worn by Federal Express employees resemble the uniforms worn by passenger airline pilots, thereby associating Federal Express with speed and therefore with speed of delivery

- Home Depot stores have a bare-bones, warehouse look to support the brand image of value

- In the mid-1990s, Cathay Pacific Airlines conducted a complete redesign of its plane interiors, ticket offices, and lounges to project a brand image of an airline that is modern, international, and yet distinctly Asian

- Alitalia Airlines has taken a number of steps to establish an upscale image, such as having its crew uniforms designed by Armani

- Companies in some product categories (for example, cosmetics) can have infomercials and other videos that directly reinforce the company's advertisements in the mass media

Another issue is that the shopping environment is perceived using all five senses, and much of this is unconscious. Note that this has implications for the issues just addressed. That is, all five senses play a role in (1) making the shopping occasion a positive one, (2) influencing mood, and (3) assisting in communicating brand image during a shopping occasion.

The customer loyalty studies of most companies usually omit macro characteristics of the shopping environment, such as the convenience of the store and the amount of parking, because those issues were addressed at the time that a site decision was made. But they are subject to change over time and should be monitored, albeit not as frequently as the other issues we have discussed.

> If the shopping environment communicates the same brand images as those of the company's advertising, the functional and emotional benefits provided by those images will be experienced by shopping in the store.

Discussion

We stated earlier that the customer's shopping experience should be a positive one, irrespective of brand image or other issues. Some companies are pushing the envelope in this regard by what is sometimes called "shoppertainment" or "entertailing." Some of the examples cited by Pine and Gilmore (1999) are a supermarket having live entertainment, free refreshments, and appearances by celebrities, and a sporting-goods retailer having a 55-foot mountain on-site so that customers can try out mountain-climbing gear. Another example is a clothing retailer giving preteen girls an opportunity to "play dress-up."

Some companies take this further. Nike retail outlets under the name Niketown are almost like sports theme parks, with video screens showing sporting events and sections of the store with flooring and walls like those of basketball courts. Another instance is an outfitter of outdoor gear having a 35-foot mountain with a waterfall inside its store, approximately 700 stuffed animals, large pictures of animals from different continents in each room, and three aquariums. Gilmore and Pine (2002) even cite retail stores that include entertainment for which the customer pays admission.

I have some reservations about this. One general reservation is that it has not been studied very much. Another reservation has to do with breadth of application. That is, can shoppertainment/entertailing be effectively established in stores of most product categories? It is easy to see how this can be applied in retailers of goods that are designed to be fun (for example, hobby stores and restaurants). But what about financial services, supermarkets, hardware stores, automotive service facilities, and so on? A *Wall Street Journal* article (Kim 2006) reported that several financial institutions are pursuing shoppertainment/entertailing options; for example, PNC Bank plans to unveil more than 40 branches with Internet cafés and coffee bars.

Assessing the effect of shoppertainment/entertailing is complicated by the fact that it is conceivable that it may not influence customers' attitudes toward the company, but still may induce them to visit the store more frequently or spend more time there on a given shopping occasion, which may increase purchase volume.

Time will tell.

E-COMMERCE

E-commerce has the following aspects, most of which pertain to the Web site:

- Creditability (for example, customer testimonials)

- Ease of use

- Features and benefits (for example, side-by-side product comparisons)

- Purchase process

- Security and privacy

- Telephone service and support

- Dialogue

- Aesthetics

As in the case of a brick-and-mortar store, the look and feel of the Web site should communicate the brand images that the company is trying to maintain.

It is too early in the life of e-commerce to say with any certainty, but conceivably the Web site may have a strong effect on loyalty. One reason is that the interactive nature of the usage process enables the company to tailor its communications, including marketing communications, to the individual user while he or she is shopping. Those communications can be as numerous and lengthy as desired by the customer, and they can be multimedia.

Another reason that the Web site may conceivably have a strong effect is that the interactive nature of the usage process establishes a dialogue between the user and the company, and therefore a rudimentary relationship. Theoretically, the company can enhance that dialogue and relationship in many ways, such as contests and user polls on issues related to the product/service category.

A Web site also gives the company an opportunity to establish a user community. This can be accomplished by establishing chat rooms, bulletin boards, and other forums. However, there is a wild card: the company has only limited control over what people say to each other in these forums, and so the effect on customer loyalty may even be negative in some individual cases. There is also the question of the extent to which users will associate the community with the brand in a way that will lead to loyalty.

Conceivably, the effect of the Web site on loyalty may be large for several reasons—marketing communications tailored to the individual customer while he or she is shopping, establishment of a dialogue and relationship with the user, and the opportunity to establish a user community.

RELATIONSHIP

There is a theme, sometimes by name and sometimes not, that runs through some of the recent books and articles about customer loyalty. That theme is relationship.

In some instances, this is the "R" in CRM (customer relationship management). In other instances, authors are referring to something else: the emotional bond between the customer and the company. We will address the latter here.

How can a company establish and maintain an emotional bond with its customers? The answer is obvious in many business-to-business product categories: develop *friendships* with your clients. This is feasible because the number of clients, especially important ones, is so small that the seller can spend a significant amount of time with each client. Consequently, the seller can learn about the individuals on the buyer side with whom they deal and then record that information—their children's names, how they like to spend their free time, what types of books or movies they like, and so on. The seller can then research those areas, enabling him or her to engage in small talk with the people on the buyer side, make gestures such as getting tickets to hard-to-get sporting events or musical events, or tell the person where to purchase vacation packages to particular places.

But in most business-to-consumer product categories, the number of customers is so large that this is not possible. What can those companies do to strengthen their relationships with customers?

One possibility that has been suggested is CRM. That is, use information technology (IT) to tailor products/services and marketing communications to the individual customer. However, in spite of the frequency with which this is discussed, it is not feasible in most business-to-consumer situations. The immediate obstacle is that few companies maintain purchase information at the individual customer level and consequently do not know the identities of their customers.

In most product categories, the only exception to this is customers who pay using the store charge card or who are members of the store's reward program (for example, airline frequent-flier programs). Furthermore, not all companies that have reward programs maintain purchase behavior records at the individual customer level.

But there is a solution available. This chapter has identified three things that any company can do to strengthen its relationship with its customers: (1) satisfy fundamental human needs during the service process, (2) provide emotional benefits through brand image, and (3) empathize.

MARKETING COMMUNICATIONS DESIGNED TO INCREASE CUSTOMER LOYALTY

The purpose of marketing communications has traditionally been the acquisition of customers, not the retention of customers. We discussed earlier that while traditional marketing communications influence brand image and thereby influence loyalty among customers, this is an unintended effect, as those advertisements are usually designed to acquire customers. But this suggests a question: should some marketing communications be designed specifically to increase the loyalty of existing customers?

In some business-to-business industries, this has been done for many years. Indeed, communications vehicles (company magazines, newsletters, and company videos) aimed at current customers have been developed especially for this purpose.

But this idea is new in many business-to-consumer categories. It would seem to warrant consideration, at least. One reason is that research has found that customers of a given brand tend to be more attentive to that brand's advertisements than noncustomers.

This raises the question of what the content of such communications should be. Should it be the same as that for noncustomers? Certainly, the communications should support the image of the brand the company is trying to maintain. That said, one of the reasons for customers' greater attentiveness to the company's marketing communications is that they are unconsciously trying to obtain confirmation that they made the "right" choice. Given that, perhaps a company should use its marketing communications to meet this desire. Such marketing communications would need to focus on the rational or functional benefits of the product/service.

In the case of consumer services, a company may want to consider using the communications to remind the customer (consciously or unconsciously) of how the company's service satisfies the human needs we discussed earlier (security, self-esteem, justice). I do not know of any companies that have used these strategies in designing marketing communications, but they do seem reasonable.

As mentioned earlier, marketing communications vehicles targeted at current customers have been used in business-to-business for years, but are now sometimes being used in business-to-consumer settings. Some companies that collect their customers' contact information send them fliers and catalogs.

Saturn has a more elaborate marketing communications vehicle. It holds "Saturn Factory Homecomings," at which customers meet the workers in the plant, eat barbecue, and talk with other Saturn owners.

CONCEPTUALIZING THE ENTIRE CUSTOMER EXPERIENCE FOR MANAGEMENT PURPOSES

A company must conceptualize the customer experience and its components in a form that enables the company to manage that experience. The customer experience as conceptualized in this book has the following components (factors):

- Product quality

- Service at each service channel (including empathy and meeting fundamental needs)

- Price

- The shopping environment (defined broadly to include everything in the store except service provided directly by employees)

- Brand image

These factors influence attitudinal loyalty, which then influences repurchase behavior. (Technical readers should note that the term "factor" is not being used here in the sense of factors in the factor analysis analytical technique.) The interrelationships between these forces are depicted graphically in Figure 1.2.

Recognize that even this complex picture is a simplification. The direction of influence involving brand image is usually going both ways; for example, product quality influences brand image, and brand image influences perceived product quality. The former direction is usually stronger in most product categories.

In practice, the service aspect of this conceptualization must sometimes be modified. If only a very small percentage of the company's customer base uses a given service channel, users of that channel will necessarily

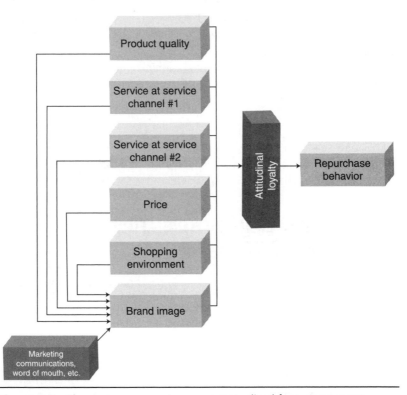

Figure 1.2   The customer experience conceptualized for management purposes.

compose a very small percentage of a survey sample representative of the company's customer base. The percentage may be so small that even a large survey sample will not contain enough users of that channel to provide enough evaluations of the company's performance for analysis purposes. In such situations, it may be necessary to combine service channels in the analyses of customer experience research data.

2

Collection of Information

Certain information is necessary for managing the customer experience. This chapter identifies that information and describes how it can be obtained.

PREFACE

When used in the remainder of this book, the term "customer loyalty" refers to an attitude having behavioral consequences. Specifically, *customer loyalty* is a favorable attitude toward a company/brand or its products, leading to repurchase behavior. There are other terms that may be more accurate descriptions of this concept (for example, "psychological attachment"), but "loyalty" will be used here in order to be consistent with the industry.

BACKGROUND

Given that our ultimate interest is in repurchase behavior, the question may be asked, Why study attitudinal loyalty; why not study repurchase behavior? The most common reason is that while behavior sometimes affects attitude, the direction of influence is usually more in the other direction; that is, attitude affects behavior. Because of this sequence, attitudinal loyalty measurements can be used as an early warning system by the company.

An early warning system is needed because customers who are dissatisfied with a company may nevertheless stay with that company because of particular circumstances, and those circumstances may change. For example, competing products may become more readily available or improve in quality, new products may be introduced into the market, or the marketing strategies or tactics of competitors may improve.

Focusing on attitudinal loyalty is especially important for product categories in which purchases are infrequent (for example, automobiles). In such product categories, several years may pass before dissatisfaction influences sales, thus alerting the company of the problem, during which time unfavorable word of mouth spreads.

There is an additional reason for studying attitudinal loyalty in many business-to-consumer industries: purchase behavior information is not available at the individual customer level. Store-level sales information is available, of course, and can be statistically related to customer survey results that have been aggregated at the store level, but drawing conclusions about customer motivation on this basis is problematic. There is a host of statistical problems. Indeed, if a store's sales increase, we don't even know if that is because the number of customers has increased, or that existing customers are buying more. In addition, there are problems of a conceptual nature; perhaps the most fundamental problem is that a store's customers do not make purchasing decisions collectively, but individually.

INTRODUCTION

Only a small portion of the information necessary to manage the customer experience is produced as a by-product of company operations. Most of the information must be obtained from a research program designed for this purpose. As background for this and later chapters, the objectives and tasks of such a program are:

- Measure the loyalty of your customers and your competitors' customers.

- Measure your performance and that of your competitors on the components (factors) that compose the customer experience. Those factors are product quality, service at each service channel (for example, brick-and-mortar retail store, telephone help line), price, the shopping environment, and brand image. Recall that "shopping environment" is broadly defined to include everything in the store except service provided directly by employees.

- Among your customers, measure the strength of influence (on loyalty) of the previously mentioned factors.

- For each factor, identify its attributes (for example, reliability and durability in the case of product quality), your performance on them, and their strength of influence on the respective factor.

- Obtain your customers' evaluations of your performance and that of your competitors at the brand image attribute level.

- Deploy the study results within the company.

- Monitor progress.

- Identify products or services that are not currently provided by you but are desired by your customers.

Different types of research studies are required to achieve these objectives.

TYPES OF RESEARCH

Broadly speaking, social research studies can be classified as either qualitative or quantitative. To illustrate, focus groups are qualitative research, whereas the results of political polls that we often see reported in the media are quantitative research.

> Quantitative studies are better suited for performance assessment and obtaining somewhat general guidance in improving your performance. Qualitative research is better suited for obtaining depth of information.

The key difference between the two types of research is that the results of a quantitative study are projectable to a larger population of interest—your customer base, in our case—but those of a qualitative study are not. For example, if 32 percent of the people in the study are loyal, we can say that 32 percent of the company's customer base is loyal, plus or minus 5 percentage points because of sampling variability.

One of the characteristics that makes a study's findings projectable is a sufficient number of respondents. Many researchers regard 150 as a minimum number unless the customer base is small. Related to this, another requirement is that the customer sample be representative of the larger population of interest (your customer base).

Another characteristic that makes a study's findings projectable relates to the questions that are asked of the respondents. In a quantitative study, everyone is asked the exact same questions and selects an answer to each question from a set of possible answers predetermined by the study designer. This is key because it is the aggregate responses to these questions (for example, the percentage of respondents who say they are "highly satisfied") that we project to the total customer base. Qualitative research differs in that the interview and the customer's responses are more complex, and there are far fewer respondents.

In customer research, quantitative studies are better suited for performance assessment and obtaining somewhat general guidance in improving customer loyalty. For example, 40 percent of your customers give your service people low scores on responsiveness. Qualitative research is better suited for obtaining depth of information. For example, are your service people less responsive to certain types of customer needs than others, and what specific behaviors need to be changed and how?

OVERVIEW OF A CUSTOMER EXPERIENCE RESEARCH PROGRAM

The design of the studies that compose a customer experience research program differs to some degree from one product category to another, and it may differ from one company to another within a product category. However, it is possible to describe those studies in general terms. This applies not only to service-oriented companies (for example, fast-food restaurants), but to any company that provides services to its customers as one of its activities.

The studies that make up the research program are as follows:

- Research to identify the attributes of each factor composing the customer experience
- Transaction study
- Qualitative research to support the transaction study
- Relationship study
- Strategic research of your customers
- Attrition analysis

These studies are discussed in the following sections.

> We have heard the expression, "The whole is greater [in utility] than the sum of its parts." This should be the case in a customer experience research program. The opposite can also be true; unless the individual studies are designed with the other studies in mind and the manner in which their results will be used, the program can be *less* than the sum of its parts. Indeed, it probably will be.

Research to Identify the Attributes of Each Factor Composing the Customer Experience

It was argued in Chapter 1 that most existing customer loyalty research programs do not address all the facets of the customer experience. But that does not mean that the facets those studies do address are unimportant. Indeed, many of them are very important. This is especially true of service in brick-and-mortar facilities and product quality.

A substantial amount of work has been done over the years in traditional customer satisfaction research and customer loyalty research to identify the attributes that make up product quality and service quality. Garvin (1988, 49) developed the following list of product quality attributes:

Performance

Features

Reliability

Conformance to advertised specifications

Durability

Serviceability

Aesthetics

Perceived quality

In some cases, ease of disposal and the package in which the product is sold should be added to this list.

There are some product categories in which *use* of the product provides emotional benefits common to all the products in the category, regardless of brand image. An obvious example is motorcycles. A list of emotions that focus specifically on use is shown in Table 2.1.

Zeithaml, Parasuraman, and Berry (1990, 21–22) developed the following list of service quality attributes:

Tangibles (for example, appearance of the store)

Reliability

Responsiveness

Competency

Courtesy

Credibility

Security

Accessibility

Communications skills

Understanding the customer

Table 2.1   Emotions experienced during use/consumption.

Anger	**Love**
Frustrated	Loving
Angry	Sentimental
Irritated	Warmhearted
Discontent	**Peacefulness**
Unfulfilled	Calm
Discontented	Peaceful
Worry	**Contentment**
Nervous	Contented
Worried	Fulfilled
Tense	**Optimism**
Sadness	Optimistic
Depressed	Encouraged
Sad	Hopeful
Miserable	**Joy**
Fear	Happy
Scared	Pleased
Afraid	Joyful
Panicky	**Excitement**
Shame	Excited
Embarrassed	Thrilled
Ashamed	Enthusiastic
Humiliated	**Surprise**
Envy	Surprised
Envious	Amazed
Jealous	Astonished
Loneliness	**Other**
Lonely	Guilty
Homesick	Proud
Romantic love	Eager
Sexy	Relieved
Romantic	
Passionate	

Source: M. L. Richins, "Measuring Emotions in the Consumption Experience," *Journal of Consumer Research* 24 (September 1997): 144–45.

Not all the attributes in these lists are applicable in all product categories and they may not be exhaustive in a given product category, but they do serve as good starting points for developing lists of attributes.

In some instances, the attributes will need to be broken into multiple attributes. For example, in the case of automobiles the attribute "performance" may need to be delimited into acceleration, braking, control while turning, and so on.

There may well be attributes peculiar to your product category that were not listed earlier. Identifying these attributes is among the most important tasks in a customer experience research program. It is vital to identify all the attributes that are actually important to customers; simply relying on assumptions about customers made by company dogma is risky. This recommendation is analogous to the often-cited injunction about believing your own advertising.

Identifying the attributes is accomplished by conducting focus groups of customers specifically for this purpose, talking to employees within the company who deal directly with customers, studying actual service experiences, examining research-oriented publications in your industry and in those similar to yours, and by other methods.

Readers interested in additional information on this topic can consult Chakrapani (1998), Naumann and Giel (1995), or Dutka (1995). Smith (2000) contains good background information on company Web sites.

In the case of brand image, the work has already been done for you. The brand positioning study conducted by the strategic planning and/or marketing department, described in Chapter 1, identified the relevant brand image attributes.

Regarding the attributes of the shopping environment, in some product categories many of the attributes can be identified by using the methods listed earlier for product and service quality. But in other product categories this is not the case; many of the attributes can be identified only by using specialized qualitative research methodologies. This is true for several reasons. One is that the shopping experience is multisensory, and most of us don't have experience in identifying attributes pertaining to sound, smell, and touch. Related to this, the shopping experience is partly subconscious, which makes the attribute identification task inherently difficult.

> As has been said countless times, you can't manage what you don't measure.

Transaction Study

The main purpose of a *transaction study* is to measure your service quality *at each organizational unit* of a given service channel (for example, each branch of a bank).

The questionnaire solicits evaluations of your service at the customer's last transaction, in terms of (1) overall service quality, (2) each service attribute (including human needs), and (3) empathy.

The service evaluations are obtained for each organizational unit and are reported quarterly to the manager of the respective unit. I recommend that even though the evaluations are reported quarterly, they should be collected monthly. The reason for monthly collection is so the quarterly report reflects the unit's performance over the entire quarter, not just one month of the quarter, which may be atypical. (Admittedly, arguments can be made for conducting all the interviews in the last month of the quarter.)

The reason that service evaluations are needed for each organizational unit, and relatively frequently, is that service evaluations exhibit a large amount of variation. The amount of variation is large in several respects— between organizational units of the same service channel (for example, bank branches), between service channels (for example, bank branches and telephone service centers), and over time for a given organizational unit.

One reason for the large amount of variation in service quality compared with product quality is that service is not mechanized nearly as much as the manufacturing of products, and people are not as consistent (from one person to another and over time) as machines.

Another reason is that in most respects, service quality cannot be checked before the customer receives it, whereas product quality can. Almost all manufacturing plants have quality-control programs capable of detecting tiny deviations from specifications.

You will probably need multiple transaction studies, one for each service channel. The reason for having multiple studies, rather than having only one study and asking all the respondents to evaluate all the service channels, is that a given customer may use only one service channel.

In some product categories, there are multiple service-person contact points in one service channel, and a customer may use more than one of them on one occasion. For example, in some financial services companies, a customer may, in the same phone call, deal with the help-line service person and the customer service manager. In such a situation, the respondent will need to separately evaluate the company's performance at each of those contact points.

In product categories in which products are prepared or assembled at the service channel unit (for example, fast-food restaurants), *product* quality may vary for the same reasons that service quality varies. It will usually not vary as much as service quality, but the variation may be of sufficient magnitude to warrant inclusion in the study.

In some product categories, the nature of the shopping environment is such that its quality can vary to a meaningful degree from one organizational unit to another. In this situation, the questionnaire should contain shopping environment questions at the overall level and at the attribute level.

The interview should be conducted as soon after the service experience as possible. This is because customers' memories of a transaction fade rapidly in most product categories unless the transaction was much better or worse than expected.

An Alternative Design

If the number of attributes is substantial, you may benefit from using two versions of the transaction questionnaire: the short version and the long version. The long version is what was just described.

The short version contains only the overall service evaluations at the contact points and perhaps high-level attributes (for example, vehicle performance). The short version is used for three-quarters of the year and the long version for only one-quarter.

A benefit of this research design is that it will reduce the burden on respondents in total. In addition, it may lower costs of data collection, analysis, and reporting. The reduction in data collection costs may be substantial if automated telephone interviewing (IVR) is an option for your company, as the short version of the questionnaire is short enough to be administered by IVR.

This research design has an additional benefit in product categories in which products are prepared or assembled at the service channel unit (for example, fast-food restaurants). In such product categories, product quality may not vary as much as service quality and therefore may not need to be measured as often (quarterly, for example), but it does vary enough to warrant yearly measurement.

A disadvantage of this research design is that responses to a given question in an interview may be influenced by preceding questions, and consequently the responses to a question in the short version may not be comparable with responses to that question in the long version. A similar situation exists in comparing evaluations obtained using IVR with those obtained by some other method of questionnaire administration. It may be possible to adjust the responses to make them comparable, however.

Qualitative Research to Support the Transaction Study

Suppose that an organizational unit has a relatively low performance evaluation on a certain attribute. Exactly what should the manager of that unit do to improve his or her unit's performance on that attribute? Of all the questions voiced by users of customer research, this is one of the most common. It is also one that most customer research programs handle poorly. I recommend several endeavors especially designed to answer this question.

We begin by grouping the organizational units on the basis of similarity of conditions that may directly or indirectly influence service. If we use a bank as an example, one group might be bank branches in rural areas in the Midwest.

After these groups have been created, a few service managers from each group visit several stores in their respective group. Pretending to be customers, the service managers study interactions between service people and customers. A purposeful effort is made to identify and focus on interactions that pertain to the attribute questions in the transaction questionnaire.

Admittedly, if this is not done with tact, employees will regard this as spying and the damage done will outweigh any benefit that is obtained.

The stores selected for this research should include both high-performing and low-performing stores. This gives us the opportunity to compare the two groups of stores and to develop tentative explanations for differences in attribute performance.

In addition to the in-store observations, discussions are held with managers of stores whose scores have improved for the purpose of learning exactly what those managers did that they believe caused the improvement. This information is especially valuable because it is the most actionable type of information readily available.

Talking to the manager of an organizational unit that has always had high performance will probably not yield as much insight as one might think. By definition, such a manager did not take steps that caused a performance improvement.

In addition, qualitative research is conducted among customers. This consists partly of research focusing on customer feelings. There are qualitative interviewing techniques from the field of psychology that have been adapted especially for this purpose—for example, one-on-one interviews in which the interviewer shows the respondent pictures or videos of service experiences and asks the respondent what he or she believes the customer is feeling.

This research is infrequently conducted, perhaps every one or two years.

Relationship Study

As its name implies, the *relationship study* is designed to measure the loyalty of customers, to cover all aspects of the customer experience with the company, and to reflect the cumulative effect of all of the customer's contacts with the company over the previous year. Another purpose is to obtain information on the performance of competitors.

Both your customers and your competitors' customers are interviewed. Customers evaluate their respective company's performance on each factor, at the overall and attribute levels. With the exception of brand image, a respondent evaluates only his or her company. In the case of brand image, your customers evaluate your performance and your competitors' performance; this evaluation is at the overall and attribute levels.

In some product categories and populations, customers tend not to perceive any differences in brand image among competitors, or differences from one attribute to another for a given competitor. If the study cannot be designed to avoid this, the best course of action may be to ask the respondent to evaluate only his or her company.

Note that by collecting performance information on your competitors, you have a basis for determining whether your scores are low or high. Of equal importance is that this is the appropriate standard of comparison. In recent years, some companies have been making what I regard as bizarre comparisons, such as financial institutions comparing their loyalty scores with those of high-tech telecommunications companies. This makes no sense to me, given that a customer dissatisfied with a bank will not replace it with a pager. Our ultimate focus should be on repurchase behavior.

> The transaction study is for service managers at the individual organizational unit level. The relationship study is for senior and middle management.

Strategic Research of Your Customers

One purpose of strategic research of your customers is to identify products or services that are not currently offered by you but are desired by your customers. It is through this type of study that, for example:

- A rug cleaning company learns that customers will have their rugs cleaned more often if the company picks up and returns the rugs.

- A truck rental company learns that it can sell products that are needed by people who are moving (such as boxes, box tape, adjustable nylon straps).

- A motorcycle manufacturer learns that it can acquire more customers if its dealers offer training courses to new motorcycle riders.

- A hardware store learns that it can sell a larger number of heavy or large products if it offers on-site truck rentals.

Obviously, thinking outside the box is essential in this type of study.

Note that without this research, you can do well the things you do, but still lose customers because you are not doing all the right things.

Another purpose of this research is to identify competitors from *outside* your distribution channel or your product category as you define it. For example, telephone companies compete with cable TV companies because both are providers of Internet access; some PC mail-order companies also sell digital cameras and therefore compete with brick-and-mortar camera retailers; and some supermarkets compete with convenience stores by offering quick checkout and beverage racks close to checkouts.

Some of the quickest company declines in history occurred when the company became aware too late of competition from outside its product category.

> You can do well the things you do, but still lose customers if you are not doing all the right things.

Attrition Analysis

In most cases, especially in business-to-consumer product categories, you will not obtain very much accurate information by asking customers who have left the company to explain their reasons for doing so. Customers in such an interview usually try to appear rational or otherwise justify their behavior.

Another obstacle in many business-to-consumer categories is that the company does not know when it loses a customer. Related to this, a customer would need to be interviewed within a few weeks of leaving, while he or she is able to remember the reasons for leaving.

These problems can be avoided by conducting qualitative research of customers who, in the transaction or relationship studies, gave low overall evaluations. (We are assuming that these people are roughly representative of customers who have left the company.)

Some companies interview customers who have registered a complaint with the company's formal complaint system, using them as surrogates for customers who have left the company. There is a problem with this. People who complain usually do so because of anger or frustration; therefore, they are more likely to complain about certain aspects of service quality than others. They may differ from the customer base as a whole in terms of demographics, purchase patterns, and personality. As a consequence, they may not be representative of customers who leave the company. Furthermore, in many product categories, most dissatisfied customers don't register a complaint with the company's formal complaint system.

AN OBSTACLE

In most business-to-consumer product categories there is a formidable obstacle to conducting the studies we have described: the information we need in order to contact the customer and conduct the interview is not readily available. Or it may be available for only some customers, who may differ in relevant ways from those for whom the information is not available. That is, the available customers are not representative of all of the company's customers.

In most business-to-business product categories, contact information is readily available on all of the company's customers because the company necessarily collects and maintains that information in the course of operating the company. But this is not the case in most business-to-consumer product categories. What should these companies do?

The answer depends to some extent on the study. In the case of the transaction study, we not only need contact information on the customers, we need to be made aware when they make a transaction so that we can interview them soon afterward. An option available to some companies is to interview holders of the store's charge card. Another option is to interview members of the company's customer reward program (for example, frequent-flier programs in the airline industry). But the company's information collection system must be such that the company is made aware when a member makes a transaction.

Unfortunately, both of these options have a drawback: the customers are probably not representative of all your customers. That is, customers who have a store charge card or belong to the reward program differ from those who don't.

Another approach is to place a person at the exit of each of your stores and have him or her intercept every tenth (or whatever) person who made a purchase and solicit the needed contact information. However, this process is expensive because it needs to be done at each of the company's stores.

Some readers may wonder why, in the approach just described, we would not interview the customer on the spot rather than soliciting contact information and interviewing the customer later. The reason is that many customers would not feel free to give negative evaluations while they could be heard or seen by the store's employees.

Another solution is to approach the problem from the opposite direction. That is, *get the customer to contact us* for purposes of being interviewed. This can be done by programming the sales registers to randomly select people making purchases, and printing out the contact information on the sales receipts. The contact information may be either a phone number that the respondent can call for an IVR (automated telephone interview) or the address of a Web site where the customer can participate in an interview.

The store intercept and sales register approaches yield much more representative samples than the store charge card and customer reward program approaches. Admittedly, the store intercept and sales register approaches do have a problem: they are more likely to select frequent purchasers than infrequent ones. It is sometimes argued that this nonrepresentative characteristic of the obtained customer sample is actually desirable because frequent purchasers are more valuable to you than infrequent purchasers. But this depends on the product category; in some product categories, the fact that a person purchases more often does not necessarily mean he or she purchases more on a yearly basis.

In the case of products, an option available to manufacturers is to include a product registration form in the package containing the product, soliciting the buyer's name and phone number. This form is filled out by the buyer and mailed back to the manufacturer. But this approach has the same problem as just discussed: the obtained sample may not be representative of all your customers. That is, the people who return the forms may, on average, differ in relevant ways from those who do *not* return the forms.

Regarding the studies other than the transaction study, we do not have the restriction of needing to interview customers soon after they make a transaction, but the fundamental problem of obtaining contact information remains. Furthermore, this is much more difficult in the relationship study because we not only need a sample of your customers but of your competitors' customers as well. The customer identification methods we have discussed are not applicable here. For example, you can't intercept people in stores of your competitors, and you don't have access to the store charge card records of your competitors.

This is a very difficult problem. For some companies, this problem can be overcome by using a research company that maintains a multi-industry panel of customers. Some of the larger panels consist of hundreds of thousands of people and therefore they may have enough customers of each of the companies you are studying.

Another option is to ask a research supplier to establish a syndicated research program in your product category. This would enable the research supplier to use the other customer identification methods we have discussed to interview customers of your competitors. Unfortunately, many companies are reluctant to participate in such a research program because they perceive their participation would be aiding the research programs of their competitors.

There is another option open to some companies. In a few product categories, there are specialized research companies, commonly called sample list providers, that by brute force or other means have developed lists of consumers in certain product categories.

Companies in some product categories may wonder why they can't obtain evaluations of their competitors from their customers. Using a fast-food restaurant as an example, the reasoning behind this idea is that many McDonald's customers are also Burger King customers, and so if you are McDonald's you could obtain evaluations of Burger King from your customers.

The problem with this approach is that Burger King customers who are also McDonald's customers are probably not representative of all Burger King customers. For example, they do not include Burger King customers who eat only at Burger King, who by definition are Burger King's most loyal customers.

As will be discussed later, whether this is a problem depends on how the data are used. Continuing the illustration, we find that this presents a problem in obtaining an appropriate standard of comparison. On the other hand, if you are McDonald's, your customers' evaluations of Burger King's performance at the factor level have implications for which factors you need to improve your performance on.

For companies in most business-to-consumer product categories, there is no good solution to the customer contact information problem. Consequently, you have to take the best solution available and take these concerns into consideration while interpreting and acting on the results of the study.

Welcome to the research world.

DISCUSSION OF THE DEGREE OF MISREPRESENTATION POSSIBLE

We have discussed how an obtained sample may be nonrepresentative of the company's total customer base. We will use the product registration form situation to illustrate how we can calculate the possible amount of misrepresentation.

In our discussion of using product registration forms to identify customers, we said that, on average, people who return registration forms may differ in relevant ways from those who do *not* return them, and therefore they are not representative of everyone who received the form (purchased the product). But representativeness is not a yes/no condition; it is a matter of degree. The degree of misrepresentation possible depends on two factors:

- The proportion of customers who returned the form

- The degree to which the people who returned the form differ, on average, from the people who did *not* return the form, in terms of their answers to the questions in the questionnaire (or answers they would have given if interviewed)

When the "missing" people represent a small proportion of the total number of recipients of the form (everyone who purchased the product), only a small amount of misrepresentation is possible. To illustrate why this is so, suppose we conducted an analysis and then removed 5 percent of the respondents from the data file and reran the analysis. It would be mathematically impossible for the results to change substantially unless the 5 percent differed enormously from the 95 percent in terms of their answers to the questions on the registration form. But an enormous difference cannot occur in a customer experience study, because at most there are 10 points on a rating scale question. Even in a worst-case scenario in which all the missing people would have given ratings of 1 had they returned the card and all the present people gave ratings of 10—a pattern unlikely to occur—the 95 percent would not differ a great deal from the 100 percent in terms of their mean scores on the questions in the questionnaire.

On the other hand, when the missing people represent a large proportion of the total, the degree of misrepresentation that is possible increases. This is because a given degree of misrepresentation can be caused by a smaller difference between the missing and present customers in terms of their mean answers in the interview.

We have been talking about the degree of misrepresentation that is *possible*. We have no way of determining the degree to which it actually occurs, because we cannot compare the missing people with the present people, in terms of their mean answers in the questionnaire, because by definition we don't have answers from the missing customers. One possible step is to compare the demographic profiles of the present group with known demographic characteristics of the total customer base. If the characteristics do not differ to a substantial degree, it does not necessarily mean there is not substantial misrepresentation, but it may make it less likely. We can say this because, depending on the product category and population, there may be a statistical relationship between demographic characteristics and answers to questions in an interview.

ACCURACY OF MEASUREMENT IN THE TRANSACTION AND RELATIONSHIP STUDIES

Obtaining accuracy in measurement is a challenge in any consumer study. One reason is that the measurement is usually performed by asking questions of ordinary human beings with imperfect memories, who have not been specially prepared for this task.

Another reason is that in some low-involvement product categories, customers are not consciously aware of the company's service at the attribute level in many instances, even during the service experience, unless it differs from what they expect.

In order to deal with this in the interview, respondents sometimes develop evaluations of the company's performance by unconsciously making generalizations. That is, they recall the company's quality of service overall, but not at the attribute level, and so they unconsciously assume that the company performed at the same level on the attributes as overall.

In some instances, the generalization runs in the opposite direction. That is, the respondent remembers the company's performance on one attribute and generalizes to other attributes and overall.

These are some of the reasons that respondents' evaluations do not vary from one attribute to another as much as we would expect. Another issue is that respondents often have no incentive to expend much mental effort during the interview.

Telemarketers can also make things difficult. Many people dislike telemarketers, partly because of the large number of calls they receive (or have received in the past), and partly because some telemarketers make misleading statements about the product they are trying to sell. This is a problem because many people make little distinction between telemarketers and survey interviewers and decline to be interviewed.

At the time of this writing, federal legislation has been passed that greatly reduces the number of telemarketing calls, but the damage has been done. That is, people's attitudes have been established and will probably be slow to change. Furthermore, the legislation just mentioned is being challenged in court.

We may come to a time when financial or other incentives will routinely be necessary to get customers to participate in research studies and give the interview a meaningful amount of effort. (We already have to offer some type of incentive in most business populations.) This incentive may significantly increase the cost of the study.

> There is no aspect of the customer experience research program about which I worry more than obtaining accurate performance evaluations from respondents.

ADMINISTERING QUESTIONNAIRES ON THE INTERNET

When it first became evident that a large percentage of the general population would eventually have Internet access, there was a lot of excitement and optimism about administering questionnaires over the Internet. That excitement has since waned in some quarters.

One of the reasons for this decline in excitement is that customers are more likely to complete an Internet questionnaire if they receive an e-mail containing a link that sends them to the Web site containing the questionnaire. This raises the question of how to obtain customer e-mail addresses, and we have the same problems obtaining that information as with the other contact information discussed earlier.

Yet another problem, one that may become serious, is related to e-marketers and e-vandals. Many PC users employ software intended to screen out junk e-mail and virus-carrying e-mail and suppress pop-up messages. This filtering presents a problem because some of those programs operate in a way that suppresses e-mail requests to participate in Internet-based interviews.

Some e-marketers will probably try to develop methods of defeating screening software; many of the e-vandals will. The manufacturers of the screening software will respond by making their programs even more exclusive, which may have the effect of suppressing even more communications from researchers.

For these reasons, interviewing over the Internet may not become as useful for research purposes as we first expected. Only time will tell.

STRATEGIC SEGMENTATION

In most markets, buyers differ from each other in ways that are relevant to a company seeking to sell its products. They differ in terms of the functional or emotional benefits desired from the product, the amount of service needed, the desired combination of products, and so on. A company that disregards these differences and instead pursues all consumers in the market using the same approach may find itself in a situation analogous to that of the proverbial person who, in trying to satisfy everyone, satisfied no one.

In addition, buyers often differ from each other with respect to their potential value to a company. They may vary with respect to consumption volume, sensitivity to price, the financial cost of manufacturing the specific products they desire, or the financial cost of effectively reaching them with marketing communications.

Related to this is the fact that in most business markets a small portion of the buyers accounts for a large proportion of total spending in the market. This is commonly called the 20-80 rule; that is, 20 percent of the buyers account for 80 percent of the spending. Differences this extreme actually do exist in some business-to-business markets. Differences are usually less extreme in consumer markets, but they are still substantial in many instances.

For these reasons, the decision of which buyers to pursue is among the most important decisions a company will make. This decision is made largely on the basis of a segmentation study. By definition, *segmentation* is the act of dividing a market into distinct groups of buyers who desire different products/services, prices, distribution channels, or combinations thereof, or for whom different marketing communications channels or media schedules are needed.

Some of the more commonly used bases for segmenting consumer markets are as follows:

- Functional benefits desired

- Attitudes specific to the product category ("I know my hair is clean when it smells fresh")

- Personality and psychographics/lifestyle

- Behavior (usage volume, mix of products, occasions in which the product/service is used, uses for the product/service, brand(s) used most often, distribution channel)

- Demographics (life stage, age, gender, geography)

Some of the more commonly used bases for segmenting business markets are as follows:

- Functional benefits desired

- Industry

- Company size

- Geography

- Product mix

- What the product is used for

A segmentation study does not necessarily have to choose only one of these bases; in some instances, multiple bases can be used.

The segmentation analysis also provides valuable guidance in marketing communications regarding which communications channels and media schedules should be used in each segment—that is, which television programs the members of a segment tend to watch, which magazines they tend to read, and so on.

A segmentation study is usually conducted by the strategic planning and/or marketing department. Information on segment definitions will need to be given to the team conducting the customer experience research, so that the results of the customer surveys can be analyzed by segment.

The results of the customer surveys need to be analyzed by segment for several reasons. If the segments differ from each other with respect to their loyalty scores, this fact would not be discovered if the data were analyzed only at the total sample level.

In addition, the segments may differ in terms of the relative importance of the factors that influence loyalty, and this information would be needed in developing a plan to improve the customer experience.

A note about the use of the word "segment" in a broader sense: a company always segments the market in that, for whatever reason, the company's customers will differ from the total market in at least some respects. The choice the company has is whether to allow these differences to just happen, or to purposely work to acquire customers with certain characteristics.

You will go out of business if the "wrong" customers are loyal.

Technical readers should note that the data produced by the customer experience studies need to be analyzed by strategic segment. But that requires that we know the segment membership of each customer in those studies. How do we make that determination? Performing a segmentation analysis again in the customer experience studies is not appropriate because we want to use the same segments that were identified in the segmentation study conducted by the strategic planning and/or marketing department. We don't want to use the same people, but we do want to use the same segments in terms of their characteristics. This dilemma can be resolved by using the data employed in the segmentation study to build mathematical equations that classify customers into segments. The questions used by those equations are then included in the customer experience questionnaires, enabling us to classify those respondents by segment. As an aside, note that this does not require the use of all the questions used in the original segmentation analysis. A subset can usually be identified that has almost as much classification accuracy as the full (original) battery.

TACTICAL SEGMENTATION

A company sometimes unknowingly acquires customers who are different in relevant ways from its other customers. For this and other reasons, new customers need to be analyzed separately from other customers.

In many product categories there are what can be called *decision points:* situations or tenure periods in which customers are more likely to make a stay/leave decision.

For example, in consumer banking the attrition rate among checking and savings account customers is much higher among customers with less than three years' tenure. Admittedly, the bank has no influence over some of this attrition, as it is caused by lifestyle changes. People may move to a city and rent an apartment for one or two years, and then decide to either move to another city or stay and buy a home in a different part of town. But a substantial amount of the attrition can be attributed to the financial institution. Interestingly, the attrition rate may be easier to influence among new customers than among other customers. This statement is based on the fact that for some banks, the effect of overall satisfaction (with the institution) on customer retention is much stronger among customers with less than three years' tenure.

You need to identify the decision points in your product category and separately analyze customers at each point. This is because the factors or attributes that cause a person to stay or leave may differ from one decision point to another.

MEASUREMENT OF CUSTOMER LOYALTY

There is widespread recognition among customer researchers that loyalty can be better measured (and repurchase behavior better predicted) by using multiple questions than by using only one question.

Some of the reasons for this recognition are research based. One reason is statistical reliability. That is, if we were to ask a respondent the same question twice, or ask two questions similar to each other, and the respondent gave the same response both times, we would have more confidence in his or her answer than had we asked only once.

Another reason is that some questions may be good measures of high levels of loyalty but not good measures of low levels, and other questions may exhibit the opposite pattern.

Similarly, some questions may be good predictors of retention but not share-of-wallet, while other questions may do the opposite. In product categories in which products or services are frequently purchased, this is extremely important.

Other reasons are conceptual in nature. That is, there are multiple aspects to loyalty, and no one question can address all of them. For example, some researchers point to the psychological theory that motivation has three aspects—cognitive, conative (intent), and affective—and argue that loyalty should be defined using questions from each of those areas.

There is not a consensus in the industry as to which questions should be used; most researchers use some combination of those listed in Table 2.2.

One of the most frequently used combinations consists of "overall satisfaction with the brand or company," "intent to repurchase/continue," and "stated likelihood of telling others."

It can be argued that "willingness to consider purchasing competitors' products" is the single-best loyalty question and therefore should be included in any combination of questions designed to measure loyalty. But a problem is often encountered with this question in practice. The problem is that a high score (a small percentage of your customers being willing to consider other companies) is extremely difficult to attain. Consequently, this question entails a target level of performance that in practice is unattainable for most companies.

All said, the bottom line is that it is very unlikely that there is a set of questions that is the best combination in all product categories. Consequently, the decision of which questions to use to measure loyalty should be based on research among your customers in which you examine the strength of the relationship between actual repurchase behavior and alternative combinations of questions. If repurchase behavior data are not available, my judgment is that in many product categories, the best combination of three questions is probably "overall satisfaction," "intent to repurchase/continue," and some type of competitive evaluation question.

Table 2.2   Commonly used measures of loyalty.

Overall satisfaction with the brand or company	Sensitivity to price
Overall quality of the product/service	Willingness to consider purchasing competitors' products
Advocacy (stated likelihood of telling other people about the product)	Attractiveness of competing products/ services
Intent to repurchase/maintain current level of purchases	Willingness to switch to competing products/services
Willingness to continue using/ purchasing in the event of problems with service or product	Importance of the product/service category to the respondent
Willingness to expend effort/ overcome obstacles in order to purchase	Emotional attachment to the brand

Product categories in which brand image provides unusually strong emotional benefits may be an exception—there you may need to include a question that measures emotional attachment to the brand.

The reasoning behind including a competitive evaluation question is that it is more realistic. That is, a customer does not have only two choices (buy your product or buy nothing); he or she usually has at least several companies' products from which to choose, and the question should remind him or her of that.

The competitive evaluation question can measure either the attractiveness of competing products or the respondent's willingness to switch to a competitor. There is a variation on the latter version that may be better in some situations: "I am more satisfied with my current company than I would be with my *second-most-liked* company."

At the time of this writing, some companies have recently begun using a measure called the Net Promoter Score (Reichheld 2006) to measure loyalty. This score is based on one rating question: advocacy. A company should consider the previous discussion before adopting this measure. Of course, this question may have valuable application in studies of *acquiring* customers, especially in product categories in which word of mouth is important.

The formula used to calculate the Net Promoter Score also presents problems. By definition, the Net Promoter Score is the percentage of respondents falling into the 9–10 range minus the percentage falling into the 0–6 range. Consequently, *very different distributions of advocacy scores can yield the same Net Promoter Score*; for example, all of the following response distributions yield Net Promoter Scores of 40.

Detractors (0–6)	0	5	10	15	20	25	30
Passives (7–8)	60	50	40	30	20	10	0
Promoters (9–10)	40	45	50	55	60	65	70
	100	**100**	**100**	**100**	**100**	**100**	**100**

This is a problem because despite having the same Net Promoter Score, these response distributions probably differ in their implications regarding repurchase behavior. This also calls into question what conclusions we should draw from a difference or similarity between you and your competitors in terms of Net Promoter Scores.

RESEARCH COSTS

An unpleasant fact of life is that data collection costs may make a transaction study very expensive, depending on the number of organizational units. This is because the performance of each organizational unit is reported and consequently we need to interview enough customers in each unit.

Generally in consumer research (product usage and awareness studies, brand image studies, and so on), many researchers recommend that descriptions of the main subject of interest be based on a sample size in the 250 to 300 range; 150 is regarded as a bare minimum. This advice is based on sampling variability considerations.

Many companies have such a large number of organizational units that quarterly reporting of transaction study results is not financially feasible. Therefore, many companies do yearly reporting.

Another option that may sufficiently reduce the cost in some situations is the short version and the long version of the transaction questionnaire, discussed earlier.

Companies sometimes respond by going against the sample-size advice given earlier. Unless the "rolling average" reporting technique is used, the end-users of the research often become confused by the wide swings in performance scores (due to sampling variability).

The *rolling average reporting technique* obtains greater benefit from a given number of customers interviewed. Quarterly reports are based not only on interviews conducted during the respective quarter but also on those of preceding quarters as well, usually three. For example, the performance scores given in the 2006 first-quarter report are based on interviews conducted in the second, third, and fourth quarters of 2005 and the first quarter of 2006; the performance scores given in the 2006 second-quarter report are based on interviews conducted in the third and fourth quarters of 2005 and the first and second quarters of 2006.

The rolling average technique uses the data from a given customer interview in multiple reports, thereby enabling the company to conduct fewer interviews per quarter. But it has an important limitation: if a change in performance occurs, it will probably not be detected for several quarters unless it is quite large. And even that requires that the change be maintained over several quarters; if the change occurs for only one quarter, it probably will not be detected.

Whether the rolling average approach or the yearly reporting approach is better depends on the specifics of your particular situation.

Financial cost is much less an issue in the relationship study because this study is conducted yearly, and its results are reported only at the total sample and segment levels.

3

Analysis and Reporting
of Information

Different levels of management have different information needs. The information differs in terms of scope of the company's operations, level of specificity, and frequency. This chapter identifies the information needed by each level of management and describes how the data from the studies described in Chapter 2 can be analyzed to produce that information.

Senior management is addressed first, then middle management, and then lower management.

PREFACE

I have a saying—All customer experience reports are alike, in that they address the same questions: How good/bad is your overall performance? Is it improving, staying the same, or going down? What should you do to improve it? This is an overstatement, but it contains a lot of truth.

INTRODUCTION

In order to manage the customer experience, senior management needs the following information:

- A measure of the degree of loyalty of the company's customers. This is needed at the total customer base and segment levels.

- The company's loyalty score compared with that of its competitors.

- The amount of change in the company's loyalty score over time, both in absolute terms and relative to the competition.

- The performance of the company and each major competitor on the factors that compose the customer experience.

- The strength of influence (on loyalty) of each factor composing the customer experience. (Note: Some writers use the word "importance" for what this book calls "strength of influence.")

- A management decision tool that prioritizes the factors for performance improvement.

MEASURING LOYALTY

Senior management needs a measure—one number—depicting the degree of loyalty of the company's customers. This measure is needed to provide a focus for the customer experience program and to serve as a basis on which the company can assess the success of its efforts to increase customer loyalty.

The reader will recall that in Chapter 2 we recommended that loyalty be measured using multiple questions in the customer survey. This raises the question of how to combine the responses to those questions to yield one loyalty measure.

The responses elicited by those questions are performance ratings in nature. Therefore, the first decision we must make is whether to use the mean calculated across the loyalty questions as our loyalty measure or use the responses to the questions to classify respondents into ordinal categories (for example, low, medium, and high loyalty).

The mean rating approach has the advantages of being easier to analyze and easier to report. Unfortunately, it assumes that a given amount of improved performance has the same implications for repurchase behavior in one area of the mean's scale as in another. For example, we are saying that respondents with a mean of 5 differ (in their repurchase behavior) from respondents with a mean of 6 *to the same degree that* respondents with an 8 differ from those with a 9. But empirical studies have found that this is seldom the case. Consequently, most companies classify customers into ordinal categories for most purposes.

If we decide to classify respondents into ordinal categories, we have to decide on the number of categories and the definition of each in terms of the responses to the loyalty questions. These decisions should be made on the basis of actual repurchase behavior in your product category, ideally among your customers. That is, dozens of alternative loyalty classifications should be examined and the classification that most strongly differentiates among customers (in terms of repurchase behavior) should be selected.

Unfortunately, we are seldom able to fully examine all the alternative classifications we would like. The reason is that because most responses to the loyalty questions are in the middle to high end of the scales, the number of respondents falling into the lowest loyalty category is usually too low to support an analysis of that category. (This does not prevent an analysis of the other loyalty categories, of course.)

Perhaps the most commonly used number of categories is four, with those being low, medium, high, and very high loyalty. These groups are sometimes defined as shown in Table 3.1. For ease of discussion, we will refer to these loyalty categories by number, with low as category 1, medium as 2, high as 3, and very high as 4.

After deciding on a classification scheme, the company must then decide which category it will focus on. That is, which category will the company try to increase or decrease in size? *The percentage of the company's customers falling into that category is the company's loyalty score.*

Assuming that the company decides to use the ordinal category approach, another issue to be addressed is whether to give equal weight to the loyalty questions during the exercise of combining them, or whether to give more weight to some than others. If unequal, exactly how much weight should be given to each? This issue should be addressed in the examination, using actual repurchase data, discussed earlier.

Discussion

In deciding which loyalty group to focus on, several issues should be considered. Some pertain to setting goal levels of loyalty. On one hand, if the percentage of customers in group 1 (at risk) is very small and the company focuses on that group, employees will probably be content with the company's current performance and consequently not try to improve customer loyalty.

On the other hand, if the company focuses on group 4 (loyal) and the percentage of customers falling into that group is low, employees will be demoralized even before loyalty improvement efforts begin.

Table 3.1   A common loyalty classification.

Category Number	Ordinal Label	Description	Definition
1	Low	At risk	1–5 on all loyalty questions
2	Medium	Hesitant	Everyone else
3	High	Positive	7–10 on all loyalty questions with the exception of the "loyal" group
4	Very high	Loyal	9–10 on all loyalty questions

Another consideration has to do with repurchase behavior. Contrary to how it is sometimes referenced in this book, purchase behavior is not "one thing." Specifically, in product categories in which purchase volume differs from one customer to another, we need to distinguish between retention and purchase volume.

This distinction should be made for the following reason. In many consumer product categories, the customer retention rate is lowest in loyalty group 1, is substantially greater in group 2, and does not rise much thereafter. However, in consumer product categories in which products are frequently purchased, mean customer purchase volume usually has a different pattern; indeed, it may be low and relatively flat between groups 1 and 2, be somewhat higher in group 3, and be substantially higher in group 4. This is illustrated graphically in Figure 3.1.

The reader may initially be puzzled by how this graphic could have been constructed, because retention rate and purchase volume differ in their unit of measure, with retention rate being a percentage (which by definition must range between 0 and 100) and purchase volume having a different range of values that depends on the product category under study. How can both be shown on the same line chart? This is possible by using both the left and right axes of the chart, with different units of measure. Customer retention rate is positioned vertically on the chart using the axis on the left side and mean customer purchase volume is positioned vertically on the chart using the axis on the right side.

In such a product category, if you want to improve your retention rate you should probably focus on decreasing the size of group 1 and perhaps 2. Alternatively, if you want to improve mean customer purchase volume you should probably focus on increasing the size of group 4 and perhaps 3.

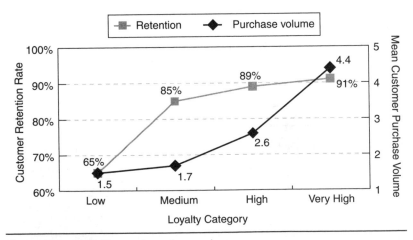

Figure 3.1 Retention and purchase volume.

If customer retention rates and mean customer purchase volume differ substantially in their relationship with loyalty, as depicted in Figure 3.1, you may have to decide which purchase behavior you will try to improve. Some of the most important issues in this decision are your current retention rate compared with the highest rate that is feasible and the cost of improving it, mean customer purchase volume compared with the highest level that is feasible and the cost of improving it, the cost of customer acquisition, and the number of customers of competitors who are vulnerable.

To further complicate matters, mean customer profitability may differ from one group to another.

> The decision of which loyalty group you should focus on may depend on whether you want to improve retention, mean customer purchase volume, or mean customer profitability.

The decision of which loyalty group to focus on has implications for the analysis that measures the strength of influence (on loyalty) of the customer experience factors. For example, if you decide to try to increase the size of group 4, the analysis should probably focus on the probability of being in group 4 instead of group 3 (or groups 1–3 combined). This analysis is a surrogate—an imperfect one—for an analysis in which we would follow customers over time and measure the strength of influence of the factors in moving people from group 3 to 4.

The question of which group is contrasted with which in the driver analysis is relevant because the relative strength of influence of the factors may depend on which loyalty groups are being contrasted. For example, the factor that has the greatest influence on a customer's being in group 2 instead of group 1 may not be the one that has the greatest influence on a customer's being in group 4 instead of group 3.

PRESENTATION OF LOYALTY SCORES

The report to senior management should contain your company's loyalty score at the level of the total customer base and each strategic segment.

Your loyalty score should be presented two ways: in absolute terms (for example, the percentage of customers in loyalty group 4) and in the competitive context. There is a presentation method that does both, as follows. Suppose that you are company B and you have two main competitors, companies A and C. You have decided that your loyalty score will be based on loyalty group 4. For each company, you would calculate the percentage of the respective company's customers who fall into group 4. Suppose those values are 21 percent, 29 percent, and 32 percent for companies A, B, and C, respectively. These values are presented in Figure 3.2.

There is another method of presentation, one in which your loyalty score is only presented relative to the competition. This method consists of dividing your loyalty score by the average of your competitors' loyalty scores. Continuing the illustration, we would divide your score (29) by the average of your competitor's scores (21 + 32/2 = 26.5), yielding the value 1.094, which would be your relative loyalty score.

Note that this score has an intuitive interpretation: the value 1.094 is saying that your loyalty score is 9.4 percent higher than that of your competitors collectively.

(Actually, it's not quite this simple. When your competitors' scores are averaged, they should not be given equal weight; they should be weighted by market share. This is very important; strangely, it is often overlooked.)

This method of presentation has an advantage over the method shown in Figure 3.2 in that it actually makes the comparison with the competition and summarizes the results of that comparison, whereas the earlier method simply enables the user to make the comparison.

On the other hand, the relative loyalty score may mask differences among your competitors (assuming that you have more than one competitor that needs to be considered). If one competitor has a loyalty score lower than yours, and another's is higher than yours, the average of these two scores

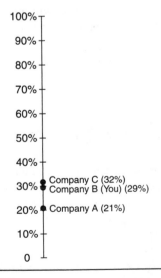

Figure 3.2   Loyalty scores.

may be equal to yours, resulting in a relative loyalty score of 1.0 and indicating parity with the competition. This may give you an unfounded feeling of security. In this situation, the earlier method should be used instead.

These methods report current loyalty scores. You also need to compare your current performance with your past performance. This can be accomplished using the chart shown in Figure 3.3. An added benefit of this type of chart is that it enables you to evaluate your performance in the competitive context.

Viewing your scores in this manner can be very illuminating. For example, in this illustration company C's current loyalty score does not differ from yours to a meaningful degree; it is only three points higher. However, the difference will probably be meaningful next quarter because company C's scores have slowly but steadily been increasing over a significant period of time (18 months), whereas yours have been practically unchanged.

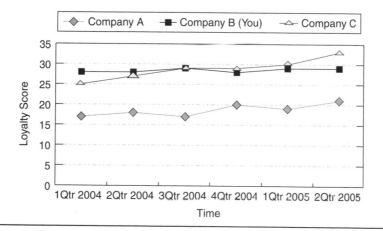

Figure 3.3 Loyalty scores over time.

PRESENTING PERFORMANCE SCORES ON THE CUSTOMER EXPERIENCE FACTORS

We previously identified the factors that make up the customer experience as product quality, service at each service channel, price, the shopping environment, and brand image. The reader will recall that the relationship study, described in Chapter 2, entails a sample of your customers and a sample of each of your competitors' customers. In each sample, respondents evaluate their company's overall performance on each factor.

In reporting these evaluations, we must somehow summarize them across respondents, as it would not be very useful to simply list the evaluations given by each respondent. This summarization is usually done either by calculating the percentage of respondents giving a high rating on a factor (for example, 9 and 10 combined) or by calculating the average rating on the respective factor across respondents.

Once calculated, these summary scores can be presented in many alternative ways. One of the most common ways, but one that I do not prefer, is the horizontal grouped-bar chart shown in Figure 3.4. Performance is the horizontal axis. The bars are grouped on the chart by factor, with each group of bars containing a bar for each company. The ordering of the factors on the page may reflect their relative strength of influence (on loyalty) or their sequence in the questionnaire.

In addition to presenting the scores graphically, this chart has the benefit of showing the actual values of the scores (7.77, 8.28, and so on). However, this chart has a disadvantage: patterns in performance involving multiple factors are difficult to identify, especially those involving a company whose bar is an interior one (company B in this illustration).

For this reason, I usually prefer another method of presentation, the vertical line chart shown in Figure 3.5. This chart is constructed in the following way. There are two axes, a vertical and a horizontal. The vertical axis

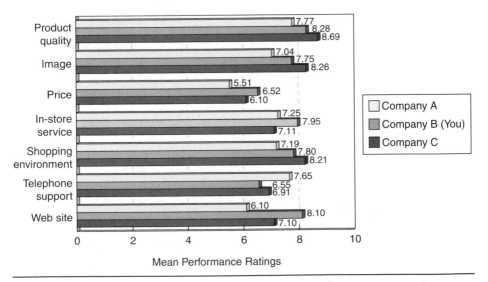

Figure 3.4 One way to present the performance scores on the customer experience factors. (*Note:* Factors have been sorted by strength of influence.)

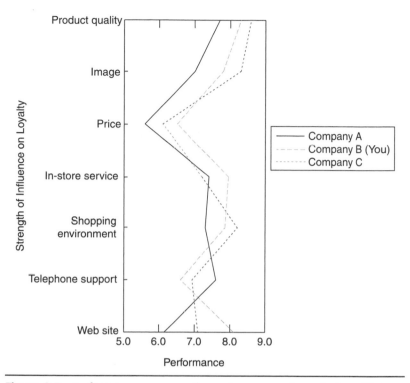

Figure 3.5   Performance scores on the customer experience factors. (*Note:* Factors have been sorted by strength of influence.)

represents the strength of influence (on loyalty) of the factors. The factors are sorted high to low on this axis. The horizontal axis represents performance. The companies are first positioned on the chart according to their performance scores on the factors. The positions of each company are then connected with lines, forming a line for each company.

Note that in actual customer experience research studies, this figure is constructed using a different color for each line. This greatly improves the interpretability of the chart. The reader is encouraged to manually make each line a different color before proceeding.

This is one of the most useful ways of presenting the performance scores of competing companies. A large amount of information can be gleaned from this chart, as follows:

- Because the factors are sorted on the page according to strength of influence, we know to give more mental weight to the top area of the chart.

- We can compare the companies in terms of their performance on each factor.

- We can compare a company's performance on a factor with its performance on the other factors.

- By comparing the lines with one another, we can identify patterns involving multiple companies. For example, company A is not performing as well as the other companies on most of the factors; no company is consistently best or worst across the service channels; and all the companies are performing poorly on price relative to their performance on the other factors.

The general rule of interpretation is that the farther right a company (line) is, relative to the other companies, the better for that company, especially if the top part of the line is to the right.

A disadvantage of this graphic (and of many graphics) is that it does not indicate whether an observed difference is real or due to sampling variability. Admittedly, another disadvantage of this chart is that if the companies are performing at almost the same levels on most of the factors, it is visually difficult to differentiate one from another. In such situations, an alternative method of presentation, such as the horizontal grouped-bar chart presented previously, may need to be used instead.

For future reference, this type of chart will be referred to as the vertical line chart.

Note that because the factors differ in nature, the same type of performance rating scale cannot be used in the interview for all factors. The factor performance ratings sometimes differ among themselves simply for this reason. In this situation, you may want to adjust the scores so that they can be more easily compared with one another. Admittedly, performing this adjustment is problematic.

A Variation of the Vertical Line Chart

Some users prefer to modify the vertical line chart so they can more easily compare their company's performance with that of the competition. This comparison can be accomplished by plotting *differences* in performance instead of absolute performance scores. That is, before the chart is constructed, subtract your score from each competitor's score, for each factor separately, and use the resulting difference values as the values on the performance axis in the chart. We have done this in Figure 3.6.

This chart is interpreted as follows. The broad line running down the middle of the chart represents you. The company on the left side of this line is not performing as well as you; the company on the right side of this line is performing better than you.

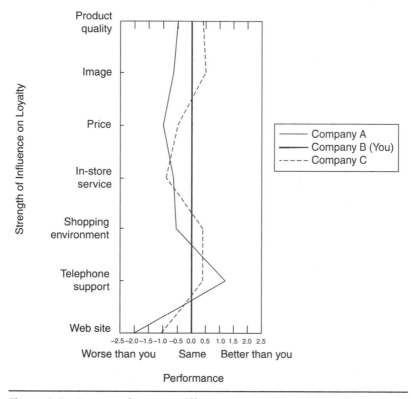

Figure 3.6   Factor performance difference scores. (*Note:* Factors have been sorted by strength of influence.)

There is a disadvantage to using difference scores instead of absolute scores. It is that we cannot identify factors on which no company is performing well relative to its performance on the other factors. This is the case because the performance scores have been centered within the respective factors.

THE SPECIAL CASE OF BRAND IMAGE

Unlike some of the other factors, simply having a high performance score on overall brand image (indicating attractiveness) is not sufficient; differentiation from competitors in terms of brand image content is very important. For example, even if you have a very high overall brand image score, you have a problem if you are perceived as being "just like" three or four of your competitors.

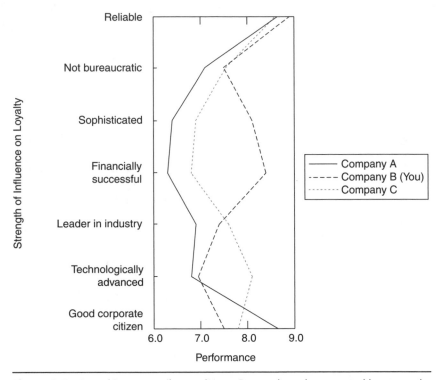

Figure 3.7   Brand image attributes. (*Note:* Factors have been sorted by strength of influence.)

For this reason, we must examine not only the overall attractiveness of your brand, but also the degree to which your customers perceive it to differ from competitors with respect to brand image attributes. The vertical line chart, discussed previously, can be used to examine differentiation. An example is shown in Figure 3.7.

PRIORITIZING THE FACTORS FOR ACTION BY SENIOR MANAGEMENT

The vertical line charts provide a picture of your performance in the competitive context, at the factor level. This is necessary information, but you also need something specifically designed to prioritize the factors for management action. Such a decision tool is shown in Figures 3.8 and 3.9. The two maps are alike except that the competitor with which you are compared differs.

For future reference, we will call these maps 3×3 competitive maps. The maps are described as follows.

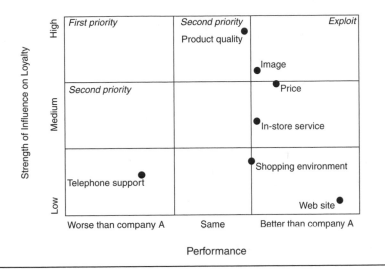

Figure 3.8 You vs. company A.

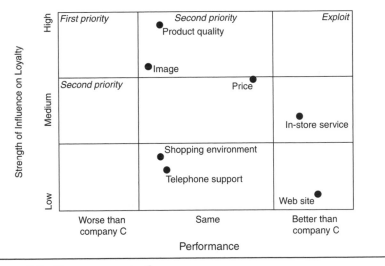

Figure 3.9 You vs. company C.

The vertical axis is strength of influence on loyalty. The horizontal axis is the *difference* in performance between you and the respective competitor. The factors are positioned according to their values on these two axes.

The vertical axis is divided into three parts of equal size. The horizontal axis is divided into three parts of *un*equal size. Factors appearing on the left side of the map are ones on which you are not performing as well as the competitor. Factors appearing in the middle are ones on which your performance is equal to that of the competitor, after sampling variability is taken into account. Factors appearing on the right side are ones on which you are performing better than the competitor.

By dividing the two axes in this manner, the factors are prioritized for management action. For example, putting aside business strategy and any other considerations, your first priority for improvement should be a factor that has the strongest influence on loyalty and on which you are not performing as well as the competition.

The different areas of the maps have been labeled in terms of priorities, but this is done merely to help orient the reader. In reality, the positions of the factors cannot be interpreted in a mechanical manner; they must be interpreted in light of your business strategy and those of your competitors. For example, if your business strategy is to differentiate yourself on in-store service, achieving parity performance with the competition on that factor is worrisome, whereas parity performance on another factor may not be.

Over-the-counter medication is an example. In some markets, the product quality of store brands is rated lower than that of other brands, and yet the store brands have substantial market share. What is the explanation for this apparent contradiction? The store brands have decided to compete on the basis of price and are priced lower.

Recognize that this graphic prioritizes the factors with respect to how *additional* (extra) resources should be allocated. It is not saying to move resources currently being spent on factors in the second-priority areas to factors in the first-priority area.

As stated earlier, multiple 3×3 maps are constructed, one for the comparison of you with each competitor. The maps are constructed independently of each other with respect to the performance gap axis. Consequently, we sometimes encounter a situation in which two or more maps have a factor in the first-priority area, but not the same factor. In this situation, we are faced with the decision of which of those two factors should be the first priority for improvement (or whether they should be given equal priority). The answer usually depends on which competitor is regarded as the greater threat. This decision is made on the basis of the company's strategic plans, the results of this study, and other information.

> Senior management does not need any more information; they already have enough information to fill a train boxcar. What they lack is decision tools that will assist them in making strategic decisions.

Discussion

The 3×3 map as just described has been used for at least a decade. But it has a limitation: it considers only strength of influence and the performance gap. Two other criteria need to be considered when prioritizing the factors for management action: the cost of improving performance on the factors from their current levels and, in the case of service channels, the relative importance of the respective service channels to the company.

The service channels may differ in importance to the company because of the proportion of the company's customer base using the channel, the spending level of the average user, the company's strategic plans, and so on. We can modify the map to reflect this by adjusting the factor strength of influence values before the map is constructed. For example, multiply the influence values of the service channels by the proportion of company sales accounted for.

Regarding the cost of improving the company's performance, the factors will usually differ greatly among themselves. The map can be modified to reflect this. Before the data are plotted, weight the *performance gap* in reverse proportion to cost. When this adjustment is done, the horizontal axis should be relabeled as "Improvement Opportunity" to alert the reader.

This adjustment of the performance gap values may seem bizarre to the reader. The key to understanding it is to recognize that we do not need to interpret individual values on this transformed variable. This adjustment is simply a method of considering two forces simultaneously. To illustrate, if a factor is the least expensive on which to improve performance and is also the factor on which you perform worst relative to the competition, that factor will be farthest to the left on the map; if a factor is the most expensive on which to improve performance and is also the factor on which you perform best relative to the competition, that factor will be farthest to the right on the map. Factors having less extreme values on these two criteria will fall somewhere in between, positioned on the map in proportion to their values on these two criteria.

Note that absolute cost information is not necessary; relative costs are sufficient. For example, improving your performance on brand image may cost 12 times as much as improving your performance on in-store service.

This raises the question of how to obtain the cost figures. There are two issues. One is the amount of *actual* performance improvement that is necessary to achieve a given amount of perceived improvement by customers. The other is the financial cost of that amount of actual improved performance.

Conceivably, the cost figures can be obtained from an analysis of historical data. That is, you can study the effect that actual performance improvement efforts have had in the past, and their cost. Acting on this is problematic. One reason is that the steps taken to improve actual performance in the past may no longer be available. For example, an actual service improvement was achieved in the past by updating the company's computer system, but this can't be done again until new computer technology becomes available.

Another reason is that steps taken in the past may not have the same effect if taken now. This may be true because consumer expectations have changed for any number of reasons. Or it could be the case that the size of the effect depends on your current level of performance, and that has changed.

Because of this, managerial judgment is usually used to develop relative cost figures. This is done by first sorting the factors from high to low according to the cost of improving performance (from their current levels of performance). The second factor from the bottom is then compared with the bottom factor, and a relative cost difference is estimated. For example, the factor second from the bottom is 1.5 times as expensive as the bottom factor. The manager then compares the third factor from the bottom with the second from the bottom and estimates a ratio cost difference, and so on.

A decision tool should consider the following information on the factors:

- Strength of influence on loyalty

- Your performance relative to the competition

- In the case of the service channels, the relative importance of the respective channels to your company

- Cost of improving perceived performance

An Alternative to the Data Used in the 3×3 Map

The 3×3 maps we have been discussing were constructed using the customers' factor performance evaluations of their respective companies. For example, the performance scores of company A used in the map were calculated using evaluations of company A from a sample of company A's customers.

Because of this, when we interpret the 3×3 map in the manner we have described, we are making a fundamental assumption. We are assuming that at the time a customer makes the decision to stay with you or switch to a competitor (including trying a competitor), he or she perceives the companies to be performing at the levels depicted in the 3×3 map—that is, as the customers of those companies perceive their respective companies.

This assumption has routinely been made (usually unknowingly) for many years by many companies, in drawing conclusions from performance evaluations. But is this assumption correct? In many product categories that are relatively important to consumers, many consumers conduct an information search prior to making the decision to stay or leave. This search typically entails actively soliciting information from people who have used other brands, reading product reviews (for example, *Consumer Reports*), and taking other steps. In such a situation, it may be true that after having conducted this information search, your customers perceive competing brands to be performing as customers of those brands perceive them to be performing.

Product categories whose products are relatively *un*important to consumers usually differ in this respect. Here, customers often make stay/leave decisions with little thought and, consequently, make their decision on the basis of whatever information they happen to have at the time. In the case of products of competitors, this information is usually superficial impressions based on marketing communications, appearance of the exterior of the store in which the product is sold, whatever the person happens to remember from happenstance comments by users of the product, and so on—in other words, overall brand image and brand image attributes. Consequently, in such product categories the 3×3 map should use *your* customers' evaluations of *you and your competitors* on brand image attributes.

This is one of the many reasons that you need to understand your customers, in particular the consumer stay/leave decision process. A good understanding of this is an absolute requirement for successfully managing the customer experience. You cannot rely on commonly held beliefs about customer behavior; for example, some companies whose products are relatively important to their customers have a substantial proportion of customers who will switch to a brand about which they have little information.

Admittedly, asking for brand image attribute evaluations of competitors is not feasible in some product categories because customers' level of familiarity with the competition is so low. This is the case in many populations regarding banks.

Preferably, only your nonloyal customers should be used in constructing this map. One reason is that they are the customers most likely to leave you, and therefore they are the ones you need to worry about most. Another reason is that their perceptions of you and your competitors are more likely to be similar to those of customers at the time they make a stay/leave decision.

Note that the brand image attributes needed in this map are not necessarily those identified in the brand positioning study mentioned in Chapter 1. The objective of that study necessarily has an emphasis on brand differentiation and therefore it may not address must-have characteristics of the company's products (for example, product quality).

In acting on conclusions drawn from this map, you must exercise caution so that nothing is done to damage your brand image among your loyal customers.

> If your customers make stay/leave decisions on the basis of brand image, this is the basis on which you should compare yourself to the competition.

Strength of Factor Influence

When brand image attributes are used to construct the 3×3 map, the axis representing difference in performance is the difference between you and a competitor, *as perceived by your customers*. This raises questions about the other axis, the strength of influence axis.

One question is, influence *on* what? Is it influence on attractiveness of the competitor, loyalty to you, or something else? Closely associated with this is the question of influence *of* what—that is, the influence of your brand image attributes or your competitor's brand image attributes.

The 3×3 map should probably be constructed in two ways. In the first, the object of the influence—the "influence on what" question—should probably be the attractiveness of the competitor. In this instance, the answer to the "influence of what" issue is to use influence of the competitor's brand image attributes.

To illustrate, if you are Chevrolet, the strength of influence axis would be the influence of Ford's brand image attributes on attractiveness of Ford, among your customers.

In the other version of the map, continuing the automotive example, if you are Chevrolet, the strength of influence axis would be the influence of Chevrolet brand image attributes on loyalty to Chevrolet, among your customers.

Both versions of the map are needed because a customer's decision to stay with his or her current company and a decision to switch to a certain competitor are two distinct issues. They are highly interdependent but still distinct.

These maps will give you guidance both in your marketing communications and in your operations.

NEXT STEPS

We have described how senior management, by using the 3×3 map with other appropriate information, can decide on which factors (or product-related brand images) the company needs to improve its performance.

The next step is to determine which attributes of the selected factors need performance improvement. This is discussed next, with the exception of price. Price is not discussed here because it is a topic in its own right and there are books available devoted solely to the subject.

At first thought, designing a decision tool for the attributes of a given factor might seem easy; you would simply designate as first priority the attribute with the strongest influence, second priority would be the attribute with the second-strongest influence, and so on.

Unfortunately, it's not that easy. One reason is that you need to take into account your current levels of performance on the attributes, for the following reasons:

- Your current level of performance on an attribute determines the amount of improved performance that is possible. For example, little improvement is possible if you already have a mean performance rating of 9.5 on a 10-point scale.

- In many product categories, moving people from one point to another on the upper end of the performance rating scale requires greater *actual* improvements in service (or whatever) than at the middle area of the scale. That is, moving a person from 9 to 10 requires greater actual improvement than moving him or her from 5 to 6.

- A company's customer base typically contains some customers— "tough cases"—who are more difficult to satisfy on certain attributes than other customers. If your average performance on those attributes is already high, you must either get new customers or satisfy an increased number of hard-to-please customers if your average performance is to improve.

For these reasons, all other things being equal, the attribute on which you are performing the worst is the one you should designate as the first priority for improvement.

But all other things are not equal. Fortunately, there is a decision tool that takes into account the strength of influence of the attributes and your current level of performance on them. It is most commonly called a quadrant map, and an example is shown in Figure 3.10. Such a map is constructed for each factor, using the attributes of the respective factor. In the case of service channels, a map is constructed for each organizational unit, using the respective unit's performance scores on the service attributes.

Quadrant maps as traditionally constructed have two dimensions. Strength of influence is the vertical axis, and performance is the horizontal axis. The attributes are plotted as points on the map according to their values on these two dimensions. After that is done, a horizontal line is drawn across the map from the mean of the strength of influence values and a

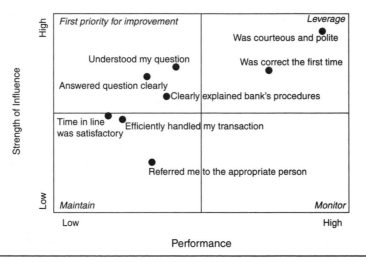

Figure 3.10   Quadrant map.

vertical line is drawn up the map from the mean of the performance values. The map is thereby divided into four sections, as described in the following table:

Levels of Influence and Performance	Customer Perspective	Management Action
Strong influence and high performance	Wants it and gets it	Leverage
Strong influence and low performance	Wants it and does not get it	First priority for improved performance
Weak influence and low performance	Does not want it and does not get it	Maintain
Weak influence and high performance	Does not want it but gets it anyway	Monitor

Obviously, the descriptions in the customer perspective column have been exaggerated here to facilitate understanding. In reality, strength of attribute influence and level of performance are not dichotomous in form; they exist in degrees.

This is how quadrant maps have traditionally been constructed. But as stated earlier, we also need to consider the cost of improved performance. We can do so using the same method used in the 3×3 map. That is, before the graphic is constructed we can adjust (weight) the performance scores of the attributes by the cost of improved performance.

Discussion

Quadrant maps have several limitations. One is that by dividing the performance axis at the mean (or median), we have in effect established that point as a target or acceptable level of performance. But there is no statistical justification for this. Nor is there justification for dividing the strength of influence axis at this point. But in order to divide the map into priority-for-improvement quadrants, we have to draw the line somewhere.

Another limitation of the quadrant map is that small distances on the map may not be "real"; they may be due to sampling variability of performance scores or imprecision in calculating attribute strength of influence. An attribute may fall into one quadrant instead of another simply because of this. Therefore, significance should not be attached to small distances on the map.

IMPROVING PERFORMANCE
ON THE ATTRIBUTES

We began this chapter by describing how senior management can determine on which factors the company needs to improve its performance. We then described how the company can determine on which attributes of the selected factors the company needs to improve its performance.

Suppose senior management decides that in-store service is the first priority, and the manager of a given store determines that her unit needs to improve its performance on the attribute "answered question clearly."

The store manager is then confronted with the question, What should I do to improve my store's performance on that attribute? Restated, What do my employees need to do?

Many customer experience programs do not address this question very well. That is why we recommended research specifically designed to meet this need, described in Chapter 2 in the section titled "Qualitative Research to Support the Transaction Study."

THINKING AND ACTING LOCALLY

Suppose that in-store service is not one of the factors that senior management decide needs improved performance. Should store managers keep doing whatever they have been doing?

Not necessarily. Senior management has made its decision on the basis of the company's average score (on in-store service). The potential problem here is that an average masks variation, in this case variation among stores. If some stores have low service scores but most have very high scores, the company's average score will be high.

Note that this is not an academic argument—in my experience, overall service evaluation scores *typically* vary a great deal from one service unit to another within the same company.

MEASURING THE PERFORMANCE OF SERVICE CHANNEL MANAGERS

It is probably inappropriate to use customer loyalty to measure the performance of a service channel, either at the individual organizational unit or at the company level. This is because he or she has no control over most of the forces that influence customer loyalty.

To illustrate, consider consumer electronics retailers. Store managers do not make pricing decisions, product design decisions, decisions as to which brands will be carried, national advertising decisions, store site decisions, and so on. The only forces that influence customer loyalty over which the store manager has influence are customer service and certain aspects of the shopping environment.

This is an issue because human nature is such that a manager will probably not try very hard to improve a score over which he or she has little control. Consequently, a service manager should probably be evaluated on the basis of his or her unit's service and certain aspects of the shopping environment.

There are two ways in which a store's overall service can be measured. One way is to directly ask the respondent to rate the store's service overall. The other way is to calculate the average of the responses to the service attribute rating questions.

A disadvantage of the "overall" question is that even though the respondent is being asked to evaluate the store's service, his or her evaluation is probably not based entirely on service. This is the case because there is a tendency for a customer's evaluation of performance on a given factor to influence his or her evaluation of performance on other factors.

The mean-attribute method also has this problem, although usually not to as great an extent. It also has the advantage of exhibiting less sampling variability than the overall service question. But the mean-attribute method sometimes has a practical disadvantage; improving performance on this measure may be more difficult for purely mathematical reasons. That is, performance on multiple attributes must be improved by a substantial amount in order to have a noticeable effect on the average of all the attributes, especially when the number of attributes is large.

Because of these issues, it is difficult to make a blanket recommendation as to which method is better.

4

Further Discussion of Analysis and Reporting

This chapter discusses management decision tools in addition to those already discussed, measurement of the strength of influence (what some other writers refer to as "importance") of factors and attributes, and other topics related to the analysis and reporting of customer experience data.

OTHER MANAGEMENT DECISION TOOLS

In Chapter 3 we described how 3×3 competitive maps can be used to identify factors or factor-related brand image attributes on which the company needs to improve its performance. We also described decision tools that identify the attributes on which the company needs to improve its performance.

Those decision tools operate by placing the factors or attributes into priority-for-improvement categories. It is possible for multiple factors or attributes to fall into the same priority category. Some users desire greater precision than this, and in the following sections we describe decision tools that attempt to provide that greater precision.

We will first discuss decision tools that do not take into account the competition, and then we will address the issue of taking the competition into account.

Priority-for-Improvement Score

There is a method for calculating what can be called priority-for-improvement scores for the factors. The factor most needing improved performance has the highest score, the factor having the second-greatest need for improved performance has the second-highest score, and so on.

The method of calculation is such that it is unlikely that two factors will have the same score. The formula used to calculate a factor's priority-for-improvement score is based on the principle that a factor's priority-for-improvement score should be proportional to the following forces:

- A factor's strength of influence on loyalty

- The amount of improved performance on the factor that is possible

- In the case of the service channels, the relative importance of the respective channel to the company

- The cost of improving performance on the factor

By "proportional" we mean the following: Using a very simple illustration, suppose that the factors differed on the cost of improving performance, but were equal to each other on the other three criteria. If one factor was twice as expensive to improve as another, its priority-for-improvement score would be half that of the other factor.

Consequently, the priority-for-improvement score tells us how to get the most bang (increase in loyalty) for the buck (effort).

Spreading the Burden across All the Factors

Spreading the burden across all the factors is a decision tool that takes a different managerial approach to improving the company's performance on loyalty. It says to improve your performance on all the factors. For example, 57 percent of any additional resources should be spent on brand image, 12 percent should be spent on in-store service quality, and so on.

Conceivably, your additional resources can be apportioned in an infinite number of ways. This decision tool considers the same four forces listed earlier in making this apportionment decision and uses the same proportionality logic. Consequently, this decision tool, like the preceding one, allocates resources so as to get the most bang (increase in loyalty) for the buck (effort).

Working toward a Goal

The decision tool of working toward a goal is similar to the one just described. It differs in that it takes into account the company's goal level of performance on loyalty. Consequently, this tool calculates how much you need to improve your performance on each factor in order to achieve your loyalty goal. An example of the results of this decision tool is presented in Figure 4.1.

There is an infinite number of combinations of performance improvement amounts that theoretically would yield the desired amount of improved performance on loyalty. For example, one combination might be 5.4 percent performance increase on product quality, 6.3 percent on in-store service quality, and so on; another combination might be 5.2 percent performance increase on product quality, 6.9 percent on in-store service quality, and so on.

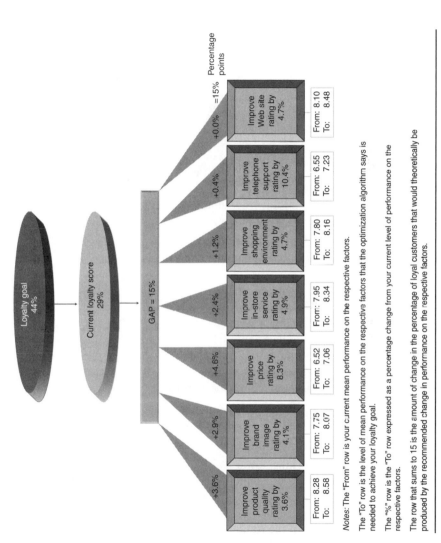

Loyalty goal
44%

Current loyalty score
29%

GAP = 15%

+0.0% = 15%   Percentage points

| +3.6% | +2.9% | +4.6% | +2.4% | +1.2% | +0.4% | +0.0% |

Improve product quality rating by 3.6%
From: 8.28
To: 8.58

Improve brand image rating by 4.1%
From: 7.75
To: 8.07

Improve price rating by 8.3%
From: 6.52
To: 7.06

Improve in-store service rating by 4.9%
From: 7.95
To: 8.34

Improve shopping environment rating by 4.7%
From: 7.80
To: 8.16

Improve telephone support rating by 10.4%
From: 6.55
To: 7.23

Improve Web site rating by 4.7%
From: 8.10
To: 8.48

Notes: The "From" row is your current mean performance on the respective factors.

The "To" row is the level of mean performance on the respective factors that the optimization algorithm says is needed to achieve your loyalty goal.

The "%" row is the "To" row expressed as a percentage change from your current level of performance on the respective factors.

The row that sums to 15 is the amount of change in the percentage of loyal customers that would theoretically be produced by the recommended change in performance on the respective factors.

Figure 4.1   Working toward a goal level of loyalty.

In calculating how much the company should improve its performance on a factor, the decision tool considers the same four forces listed earlier and uses the same proportionality logic. Consequently, the combination of performance amounts calculated by the program is the one that gets the most bang (increase in loyalty) for the buck (effort).

An advantage of this decision tool over all the others we have discussed is that it facilitates accountability of managers to a greater extent. That is, to the extent that a factor represents a particular area of the company that has a manager, the factor improvement amounts called for by the decision tool represent goals for the respective manager.

This tool can also be used for *goal seeking*. That is, by specifying alternative amounts of improved performance on *loyalty* and noting the amount of improved performance on the factors that is required to achieve this, the user can identify a goal level of loyalty that is reasonable.

A desirable aspect of all these decision tools has to do with the information that is needed on the cost of improved performance. Absolute cost-of-improvement information is not required; relative cost figures developed judgmentally, as described in Chapter 3, are sufficient.

> Although they differ in other respects, all three of these decision tools are designed to get the most bang (increase in loyalty) for the buck (effort).

The Loss of Revenue Due to Nonloyalty

Depending on the availability of customer retention and mean customer volume purchase information, it may be possible to roughly calculate the loss of revenue due to nonloyalty, subject to certain assumptions.

We will use the financial services industry to illustrate. Suppose that a bank conducts a customer survey in which the questions we use to measure loyalty are asked. As part of normal business operations, the bank maintains records of account activity for all of its customers. After an appropriate amount of time has elapsed after the survey, we can use this operations data to determine the retention status of every person in the customer survey. We can then perform an analysis to calculate the percentage of nonloyal respondents in the customer survey who left the company because of nonloyalty.

Using this percentage in conjunction with the percentage of respondents who are nonloyal and the revenue generated by the average customer, we can calculate the loss of revenue due to nonloyalty for the survey sample. This measure can then be calculated for the total customer base by simply multiplying it to reflect the number of customers in the total customer base.

Ideally, this analysis would be conducted for multiple time periods and the results averaged. For example, one would measure the effect of non-loyalty in 2000 on retention in 2001 and the effect of nonloyalty in 2001 on retention in 2002, and then average the effects. This reduces the influence of any one year, a year that may be atypical.

This information is very interesting to senior management, of course. Furthermore, we can sometimes use it to construct more sophisticated decision tools than we have discussed. Specifically, this information, together with information on the factors' strength of influence on loyalty, can sometimes be used to express *factor* strength of influence in financial terms. For example, a change in in-store service quality rating of 0.53 points is associated with a loss or gain in revenue of $50 for the average customer. Such a decision tool would, of course, make a host of assumptions, which will be discussed later.

Considering Differences between All Four Loyalty Categories

The decision tools discussed earlier treat loyalty as being dichotomous in form; that is, a customer is either sufficiently loyal or not. But as discussed in Chapter 3, in customer loyalty studies we can typically classify respondents into four categories of loyalty. In product categories in which purchase volume differs among consumers, the relationship between the *customer retention rate* and the four loyalty categories may differ substantially in form from that of the relationship between *mean customer purchase volume* and loyalty category. Figure 4.2 depicts the difference that may occur.

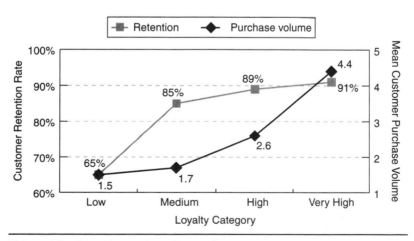

Figure 4.2   Retention and purchase volume.

Obviously, if the four loyalty categories differed among themselves to the degree depicted in this figure, a decision tool would need to take into account which categories would be most affected by improved performance on the factors. If the factors differed in this respect, this would also need to be taken into account—for example, if improved performance on service quality would reduce the size of the at-risk category more than improved performance on product quality. By making certain assumptions, we can estimate these effects.

We begin by performing an analysis that measures the statistical strength of influence of the factors on loyalty category membership. We can use an analytical technique called the Multinomial Logit Model for Ordered Dependent Categories to perform this measurement. The outcome variable in this analysis is treated as categorical in form, having four categories related to each other in an ordinal manner.

Using the equations produced by this analysis, we can perform what-if exercises. To illustrate, Table 4.1 contains the results of a series of exercises in which we increased the company's performance on each factor by one rating point while keeping the company's performance on the other factors at their current levels. Note that this increase of factor performance was made at the respondent level; that is, every respondent's rating of the respective factor was increased by one rating point.

For example, in the case of product quality the number of respondents in the loyal category increased by a number equal to 6.4 percent of the total sample; the number of respondents in the positive category decreased by a number equal to 3.6 percent of the total sample. Note that these are net results. For example, using the positive category to illustrate, these results take into account that some of the respondents in the positive category moved into the loyal category and some in the hesitant category moved into the positive category.

Most of these results make sense. In the case of every factor, increasing performance on a factor increased the size of the loyal category. With one

Table 4.1   Percentage change in distribution of total sample.

	At-risk	Hesitant	Positive	Loyal
Products	−3.1	+0.3	−3.6	+6.4
Primary Service	−0.8	−1.6	+0.4	+1.9
Price	+0.4	−2.4	−2.0	+4.0
Brand Image	−0.9	−1.6	−7.3	+9.8
Secondary Service	−0.8	−1.4	−1.0	+3.2

Note: A negative sign indicates that the loyalty category *decreased* in size; a positive sign indicates that it *increased* in size. The figures are percentages; the total sample was used as the base.

exception—price—the at-risk category decreased in size. The results for price are probably due to model estimation error.

Once we have developed the capability to estimate the effect on the relative sizes of the loyalty categories that would theoretically be produced by a given amount of performance change in a factor, we can estimate the financial consequences for the company if it improves its performance by a given amount on a given factor. Using this, there are several types of decision tools possible.

Discussion

These decision tools sound good, but they have certain weaknesses. One is that we are assuming that we have measured the strength of influence of the factors with a fairly high level of precision. (Simply placing a factor into one of the nine priority categories in a 3×3 competitive map requires less precision.) Later in this chapter is a general discussion of calculating strength of influence, but at this time we will address a problem especially relevant to the subject at hand.

As discussed in Chapter 1, in most product categories brand image influences the company's performance on the other factors, and the company's performance on the other factors influences brand image. (Remember that "performance" is performance as perceived by the customer.) Unfortunately, we have difficulty distinguishing between these two influences in the analysis.

This is a problem because in calculating a factor's strength of influence on loyalty, we need to count its total effect—that is, its direct and indirect effects. A factor's indirect effect on loyalty is its influence on other factors that influence loyalty. For example, in-store service quality indirectly influences loyalty by directly influencing brand image.

There is another problem that may arise with the use of these decision tools. In the case of the third decision tool presented earlier (working toward a goal), some users may treat the recommendations of the decision tool as predictions (guarantees). For example, if the tool says that you need to improve your performance on in-store service by 10.4 percent, and that difference will theoretically produce a 4.2-point difference in the percentage of loyal customers, naive users may think that if they increase their in-store service by the prescribed amount, they can be certain that the percentage of loyal customers will increase by exactly 4.2 points.

For many reasons, the recommendations of the decision tool should not be regarded as predictions. One reason is that the measures of factor strength of influence are almost always produced by some type of analysis of cross-sectional data, not longitudinal data. That is, we do not follow customers over time to identify those who changed their performance evaluations of a given factor and then see how much their loyalty scores changed. Instead, the analysis assumes that if respondents were to increase their ratings on a factor to a given level, their loyalty scores would rise to those of the customers currently at that level. For example, if the respondents currently giving "6" ratings on a factor were to increase their ratings to "7," their loyalty scores would rise to the level of the respondents currently giving "7" ratings on that factor.

Another reason is that the decision tool is making a host of assumptions about the future, most of which will probably not be met to significant degrees. Some of the assumptions pertain to the competition: their advertising strategy and tactics do not change, the quality of their existing products/services do not change, they don't introduce any new products or services, their prices do not change, no new brands enter the market, and so on.

> We should make clear to the users of the decision tools that the people who constructed them do not purport to have supernatural powers of foreseeing the future.

We have been discussing decision tools that do not take into account the competitive context. Modifying these tools to take the competition into account is problematic. This is discussed in the following section.

Taking the Competition into Account

We take the competition into account by calculating the difference in performance between you and the competition, in a factor-by-factor manner. The question is, which competitor should you use in this exercise? A company usually has multiple competitors.

One solution sometimes suggested is to construct an artificial competitor and use it as the competitor in the decision tool. In constructing this competitor, we give it the performance score of the best-performing competitor, on a factor-by-factor basis. That is, we give it the in-store service quality score of the competitor with the highest score on that factor, regardless of which competitor that is; we give it the product quality score of the competitor with the highest score on that factor, regardless of which competitor that is; and so on.

The problem with this is that it does not accurately depict the options available to consumers. A consumer can't choose one company's performance on one factor and another company's performance on another factor; a customer either purchases a company's product or does not, and he or she makes this decision on the basis of that company's performance on all the factors.

There are other issues to be considered, which have to do with the performance gap. One is how large the difference must be in order to be relevant to customers and whether this amount differs from one factor to another.

At the other extreme, is there a point at which increasing your superiority to the competition on a factor will no longer have an effect on loyalty? How large a gap is that? Does it depend on your absolute level of performance on the factor?

Perhaps the most difficult issue is to take into account your business strategy. Suppose that you are trying to differentiate yourself from the competition by having better in-store service. In this situation, the significance (to you) of your performance relative to your competitors differs from one factor to another. That is, parity performance with the competition on in-store service is not acceptable to you, but it may be in the case of other factors.

I know of no canned approach for satisfactorily dealing with this issue; the resource-allocation rules embedded in the decision tools discussed earlier in this chapter would have to be designed with a particular study in mind. An alternative is to construct the 3×3 maps discussed in Chapter 3 and study them in light of the company's business strategy; as has been noted by others in a variety of business contexts, sometimes the best computer is the human brain.

THE VALUE OF A BRAND

Marketers who deal with brand image have developed the concept of brand equity. Different people mean somewhat different things by the term, but I agree with Keller (1998) that most marketers would agree that brand equity has to do with the current and past marketing of the brand. Specifically, *brand equity* is the difference, in terms of sales effectiveness, between selling the product *with* the brand identification and selling it *without* the brand identification.

The idea of calculating brand equity in financial terms has received a significant amount of attention in recent years. Some attempts at calculation have been made using actual sales data. Unfortunately, those attempts may have yielded misleading results because observed differences in sales may be due to differences in actual product quality, availability of the products under study, and so on.

These problems can be avoided by using certain survey research approaches. Perhaps the easiest, albeit crude, is as follows. Suppose that you manufacture bathroom fixtures. We would ask respondents the following series of questions: "Suppose you were shopping for a kitchen sink. Suppose that a store had only two brands, [your brand] and one you had not heard of. If both brands had the same features and appeared to be of equal quality, which one would you buy if the [your brand] sink cost $50 more?" If the respondent says your brand, ask again but increase its price. Continue until the respondent says he or she would buy the unknown brand.

This exercise is also conducted for competitors of interest by replacing your name with theirs.

We can calculate the financial value of a brand by calculating the difference between the proportion choosing the brand and the proportion choosing the unbranded product and then multiplying that by price. This is done for each price level and the results are summed. This is especially useful because we can compare brands with respect to their value.

Our logic behind asking respondents to compare a brand with one they have not heard of is based on the definition of brand equity given earlier. In some product categories, using "a brand you had not heard of" may not be appropriate; in consumer package goods, "the store brand" or "a generic" may be more appropriate.

Admittedly, the results of this simple approach are rough. They are subject to the usual forces that cause a person's response to a hypothetical situation in an interview to differ from what he or she actually would do in the real world. We also have the problem of having addressed only one of the brand's products (sinks, in this case).

In addition, because the question mentions only brand and price, and varies only price, respondents probably overreact (in the interview) to the price changes. This problem can be addressed by partially drawing respondents' attention away from price by including and varying other information on the products. This can be accomplished using an analytical technique from the new product development field called discrete choice.

Brand equity is the difference, in terms of sales effectiveness, between selling the product *with* the brand identification and selling it *without* the brand identification.

CONCEPTUAL FRAMEWORK
OF LOYALTY AND ITS DRIVERS

Any analysis of customer experience data, or even a coherent presentation of simple descriptive information, requires that we have beliefs or assumptions about how the factors and loyalty are interrelated. Over the years, a dozen or so conceptual frameworks, with variations of each, have been used.

This section presents some of the more frequently used conceptual frameworks. To facilitate comparison, the framework advocated in this book is repeated in Figure 4.3.

One framework popular in the past includes "value" and places it in a central role. This framework is depicted graphically in Figure 4.4. The factors influence value, which then influences customer loyalty.

At first thought, this conceptual framework may seem appropriate because it mirrors classical philosophical writings on capitalism. Those writings conceive of consumers as "rational actors" who consciously and deliberately compare competing products with one another with respect to value, and then purchase the one having the greatest value.

There are several difficulties with this framework, however. One is that consumers rarely have complete and accurate information on all the products on the market. Even when they do, consumers seldom consider all the brands, all the models of each brand, or all the product/service attributes.

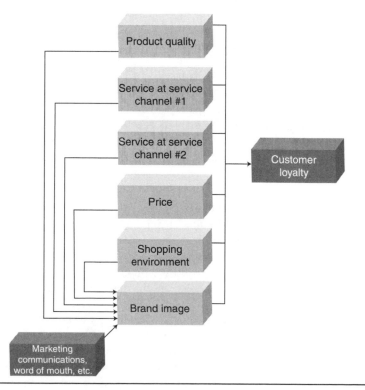

Figure 4.3   Recommended conceptual framework.

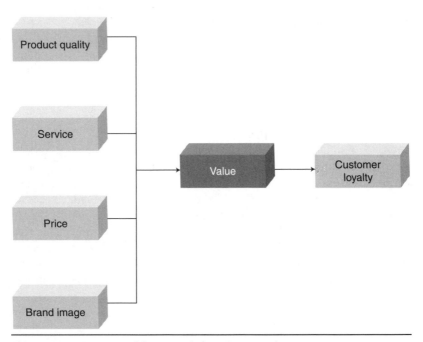

Figure 4.4   Conceptual framework focusing on value.

This happens because of the amount, complexity, and conflicting character of the information that confronts the consumer.

Another difficulty has to do with research methodology—how value is measured in this context. It is measured by a question in the customer questionnaire that essentially asks, "Was what you received worth what you paid?" We need to recognize what this question is asking the respondent to do. He or she is being asked to mentally identify the specific benefits desired from the product, determine their relative importance, and remember how well the product delivered each benefit (without being influenced by price). Then the respondent must take all that information and calculate a total benefit score, divide that by price to produce a value score, and then somehow convert that unit of measure into the one used in the questionnaire (a rating scale).

All this is expected in the half-second that interviewers give a respondent to answer a question. Not a very reasonable request, is it?

It is unlikely that respondents can answer this question with even half the accuracy and reliability with which they answer the other questions in the questionnaire. The only exception may be a business-to-business situation in which the company has a formalized performance evaluation procedure that includes the benefits desired from the product and the number of importance points of each benefit.

Another problem is that some consumers mentally associate the word "value" with only the low or high end of the quality scale. To use an automotive illustration, some people would not rate Toyota the highest on value even if they believed it had the highest ratio of total benefit to price (which is the definition of value).

It has been my experience that as often as not, when this model is tested using a structural equation approach, it is not a good model when judged by statistical measures of fit. The fit can usually be improved appreciably by specifying a model containing direct effects of the factors on loyalty.

A framework showing overall satisfaction influencing loyalty is presented in Figure 4.5. From an academic perspective, separating overall satisfaction from loyalty may make sense, depending on the conceptual definition of loyalty. But is this added complexity actually needed in practice? Furthermore, it has been my practical experience that overall satisfaction is often one of the questions needed to define loyalty. That is, overall satisfaction is often needed to give our measure of loyalty as much predictive power—predictive of repurchase behavior—as possible. Admittedly, this is probably not true of all populations in all product categories.

In the conceptual framework of loyalty depicted in Figure 4.6, factors directly influence what we may call super factors, usually psychological,

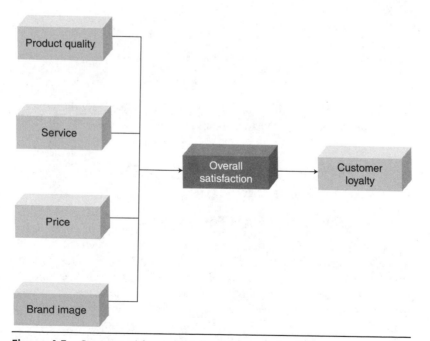

Figure 4.5 Conceptual framework breaking apart loyalty.

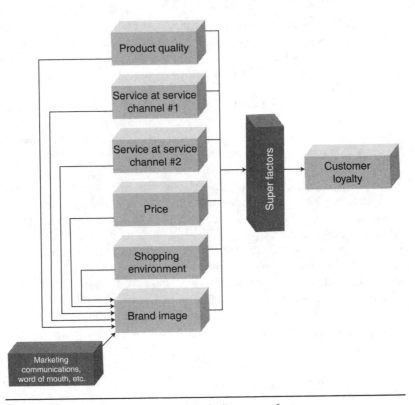

Figure 4.6   Conceptual framework including super factors.

which in turn directly influence customer loyalty. Researchers disagree as to the nature of these super factors and their identities.

MEASURING THE STRENGTH OF FACTOR AND ATTRIBUTE INFLUENCE

The Horse Sometimes Does Follow the Cart

We usually think of the relationship between attitude and behavior as one in which the former influences the latter. But the reverse is sometimes true: behavior sometimes influences attitude. A person may be attitudinally loyal in order to be consistent with his or her past and current behavior. Taking this into account when analyzing attitudinal loyalty is usually impractical, as it may require tracking individual customers over time and recording their attitudes and behavior.

Penalty/Reward Analysis

Contrary to what we have been implying in this book, a factor or attribute's strength of influence is not necessarily one thing, one continuum; it may be two or more. It is sometimes two continuums, with one reflecting the penalty effect of the factors or attributes and the other reflecting their reward effect.

An analytical approach called penalty/reward analysis has been developed to calculate the strength of these two effects. This analysis can be conducted in several contexts—for example, the influence of the factors on loyalty, or the influence of the attributes on the respondent's overall performance evaluation on the respective factor. To facilitate explanation, we will illustrate the analysis in the situation in which it has been used most often: the influence of service attributes on overall satisfaction with service.

We should first prepare the reader by noting that the analysis sees overall satisfaction as being categorical in nature, with three categories that we might call dissatisfied, neutral, and satisfied.

Penalty Effects

Consumers require a minimum level of performance on certain attributes. If the company does not perform at this level on these attributes, customers will be dissatisfied regardless of how well the company performs on other attributes. Perhaps the most common example is courtesy.

On the other hand, if the company does attain the required level of performance on all these attributes, customers will be neutral on overall satisfaction. However, further improved performance on these attributes will not move customers to being satisfied.

Restated, the company incurs a penalty for not achieving the required level of performance on the attribute, but no reward for exceeding that level. This is presented graphically in Figure 4.7.

Reward Effects

There are other attributes in which high performance is not expected but is valued. If the company does *not* attain a high level of performance on any of these attributes, customers will be neutral on overall satisfaction, assuming, of course, that the company has achieved a sufficiently high score on the necessary attributes described earlier. An example might be live music in a restaurant.

On the other hand, if the company *does* attain a high performance level on any of these attributes, customers will be satisfied.

Restated, the company does not incur a penalty for not achieving a high level of performance on the attribute, but does incur a reward for achieving it. This is presented graphically in Figure 4.8.

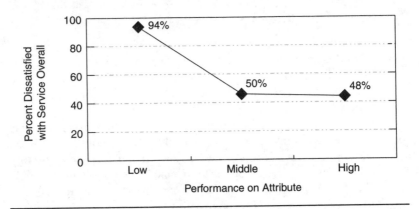

Figure 4.7 Penalty effect of attribute.

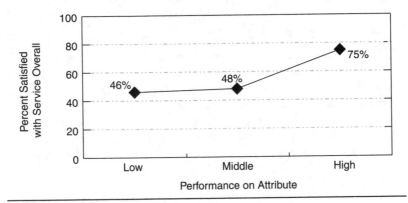

Figure 4.8 Reward effect of attribute.

Airline passengers don't care about food quality if one of the plane's engines catches fire during the flight.

Analysis

It is sometimes possible to measure the strength of these two types of influence. Dutka (1995) describes a method using cross tabs. A multivariate approach (specifically, logistic regression) will be presented here, using the same logic as Dutka.

During the analysis stage, the data must first be prepared as follows. The performance rating scale of each attribute is collapsed into three categories: low, middle, and high.

Two new overall satisfaction variables are created, each dichotomous in form; one is "dissatisfied versus everyone else," and the other is "satisfied versus everyone else."

Two driver analyses are then performed. In the penalty analysis, the outcome variable is the "dissatisfied versus everyone else" overall satisfaction variable. This variable is treated as a function of the attribute performance rating scales, collapsed as discussed earlier. In this analysis, a given attribute's influence is measured by contrasting its low group with its middle group. This contrast measures the degree to which these two groups differ in the percentage that is dissatisfied. This analysis measures the penalty effects of the attributes.

The other analysis measures the reward effects of the attributes and is the opposite of the analysis just described. That is, the outcome variable is the "satisfied versus everyone else" variable, and a given attribute's influence is measured by contrasting its high group with its middle group.

Note that there is a catch in performing this analysis. The *original* response categories of the attributes should somehow be given equal weight in this analysis. For example, suppose the attribute performance scales are collapsed so that 1–5 = low, 6–8 = middle, and 9–10 = high. In the contrast of low with high, response categories 1–5 should be equally weighted, and response categories 6–8 should be equally weighted. This is an issue because, as noted elsewhere, the responses to performance rating scales are typically not evenly spread across the points on the scale; they are concentrated in the middle and high areas of the scale. Consequently, if the original response categories are *not* given equal weight, the contrast of 1–5 with 6 8 will actually be mainly a contrast of 5 with 6–8.

Caveat

This analysis and the consumer behavior theory that underlies it make sense. And yet, as often as not, this analysis fails to find differences between the two types of effect, even when we would expect it.

The likely explanation for this is that the attribute performance ratings provided by respondents are not sufficiently accurate. The reader will recall the discussion of accurate measurement in Chapter 2.

The application of this analysis is also greatly limited by sample-size considerations. This is because simply having a large total sample is not necessarily sufficient; we need enough respondents at *each* of an attribute's performance levels. Achieving this is made much more difficult because, as noted earlier, responses to the performance rating scales are typically concentrated in the middle-to-high areas of the scale, leaving the low area relatively unpopulated.

Situation Effect

In some product categories, the data may need to be analyzed separately by use/consumption situation because the relative strength of influence of the factors or attributes, or the company's performance, may differ from one situation to another.

The restaurant business is an example. A given customer's needs differ depending on whether he or she is on a lunch break with coworkers or eating dinner with a romantic interest on a Saturday evening.

Some extreme examples are in healthcare. For example, a person with liver failure has very different expectations (or hopes) than a person with a football injury to the knee. The former will be extremely satisfied merely to remain alive.

Statistical Associations among Attributes

The attributes of a given factor are usually statistically associated with one another to a substantial degree, sometimes very substantial. (The factors are usually less strongly associated with one another.) In such circumstances it is difficult to accurately measure the strength of influence of the attributes individually.

Using an everyday example, consider the effects of parental income and parental education on children's educational levels. Both parental income and parental education influence children's educational levels. However, parental income and parental education are strongly associated statistically with *each other*; that is, most of the parents who have high incomes have high education, and vice versa. This raises the question of whether children who are highly educated are so because their parents are highly educated or because their parents have high incomes.

Stated in statistical terms, much of parental income's ability to explain children's educational levels is shared with parental education, and vice versa. Therefore, a fundamental question arises: how much of that shared explanatory power should we credit to parental income and how much to parental education?

Over the years, many statisticians and researchers, representing many fields, have endeavored to develop methods for making this decision. Most of these efforts have failed. Some appear to have had some success, but which method is most appropriate is a point of disagreement among researchers.

I believe that a different perspective on this problem is needed in some customer loyalty situations. The reason has to do with *why* the attributes are strongly associated statistically with each other. To illustrate, consider the following service questions from a typical banking study:

Was courteous and polite

Was correct first time

Referred me to appropriate person

Understood my question

Answered my question clearly

Clearly explained bank's procedures

Time in line was satisfactory

Efficiently handled my transaction

One of the reasons for statistical associations among these questions is that the company actions they represent are interdependent (not just statistically associated) in some sense. For example, "answered my question clearly" and "clearly explained bank's procedures" are interdependent by definition because many customer questions pertain to bank procedures.

Some of the questions are interdependent in a functional sense—for example, "efficiently handled my transaction" and "understood my question." How well a service person understands a customer's question affects the efficiency with which he or she handles the customer's transaction.

There is an additional kind of dependency of a different type. There is a tendency for customers' perceptions of the company's performance in one area to influence other perceptions in that area to varying degrees. For example, a customer's perception of one aspect of a bank teller's performance affects his or her evaluation of other aspects of that teller's performance.

Because of all this, if the company's performance on one attribute changes, its performance on some of the other attributes (of the same factor) will also change to varying degrees. To the extent that this is the case, it calls into serious question whether we should even attempt to measure the strength of influence of the attributes individually; we should instead somehow deal with combinations of attributes.

If only two attributes are interdependent, one method of addressing the issue is to combine the two attributes into one variable in the driver analysis.

If the interdependency is widespread, a better strategy may be to identify an optimal subset of attributes and then use only those attributes in the decision tools we have discussed.

There are several strategies for identifying the optimal subset. One is the "stepwise entry" optional feature in the driver analysis. In this feature, the attributes are entered into the driver analysis one at a time. The attribute that has the strongest influence on the outcome variable (for example, overall evaluation of in-store service) is entered into the analysis first. The attribute that, together with the first attribute, has the greatest total influence on the outcome variable is entered into the analysis second. This process continues until none of the remaining attributes would, if used, increase the total influence of the variables in the analysis.

Another strategy is to examine all possible subsets of attributes of a given number. For example, if there are 12 attributes, examine all possible combinations of 5 attributes, and then select the combination having the greatest total effect on the outcome variable.

When using either strategy, we often find that a relatively small number of attributes explains the outcome variable almost as well as all the attributes.

At first thought, we might believe that the all-possible-subsets approach is the better approach. However, a difficulty with this approach is encountered in practice. For example, the top 20 combinations often do not differ from one another in terms of their explanatory power; any observed differences in explanatory power are due to sampling variability. Consequently, we are faced with the question of which one of those 20 combinations should be used.

Admittedly, the stepwise entry approach also suffers from sampling variability, but to a lesser extent.

At first thought, it may not be clear why either of these approaches addresses the interdependency issue discussed earlier. They address it for the following reason: when an attribute is *not* being used as a driver in a driver analysis, its effect on the outcome variable is credited to the attributes that *are* being used as drivers, to the extent that those attributes are statistically associated with one other.

Using the earlier illustration, if "clearly explained bank's procedures" is included as a driver in a driver analysis and "answered my question clearly" is not included, the measured effect of the former reflects not only that attribute's effect, but the latter's as well to some extent.

Admittedly, this strategy has potential problems. One has to do with communication with managers. Specifically, managers may inaccurately conclude that attributes not in the subset do not matter and may reduce their effort on them.

Another problem is that in identifying the optimal subset of attributes, we by design are dealing with only one of the issues we need to consider in prioritizing the attributes for management action. That is, we are measuring strength of influence, but we are not considering the company's current level of performance on the attributes, the importance of the service channel to the company, or the financial cost of improved performance. Continuing the illustration, "clearly explained bank's procedures" may be a member of the optimal subset and "answered my question clearly" may not be, even though the latter may have more room for improved performance or be less expensive to improve.

> If the company's performance on an attribute will improve if its performance on another attribute improves, should we even try to measure the individual effects of those attributes?

The Problem of Nonapplicable Drivers

In the conceptual framework used in this book, the effect (on loyalty) of performance on each service channel is calculated—in-store service, telephone service associated with in-store purchases, telephone service associated with Web-site purchases, and so on.

In many product categories, few customers use all of the company's service channels and therefore few are able to evaluate the company's performance on all of them. This presents a problem in performing a driver analysis of loyalty because almost all the statistical techniques used to perform driver analyses, when applied in the manner they are typically applied, exclude from the analysis a respondent who does not answer all the questions being used in that analysis.

This is problematic because the absolute number of such respondents is usually too few to support a driver analysis of loyalty. Furthermore, such customers are probably not representative of all customers.

Fortunately, we are not the only people to face this problem. Statisticians working in other fields (for example, agronomy and veterinary medicine) have developed analytical strategies for dealing with this problem. This is not widely known within the customer loyalty community, however. Technically inclined readers should consult Freund, Littell, and Spector (1986).

Effect of the Amount of Variation in Factor or Attribute Performance Ratings

There are at least a dozen statistical techniques that have been used to perform driver analyses. They differ among themselves in important ways, but most have the following weakness: if most respondents rate the company's performance the same on a factor or attribute, the driver analysis will find that factor/attribute to have relatively weak influence. That is not necessarily true, of course.

While this may occur in many situations, it is most likely to occur in mature manufacturing industries. In such categories, the company's manufacturing processes are so advanced that, together with quality control processes, product quality is consistently high. (Of course, there is still some variation in customers' evaluations of product quality, partly because of differences between customers.)

Theoretically, this problem can be avoided by using an analytical strategy in which each point on the factor performance scale is treated individually. This strategy has two steps. The first step is that for each factor separately, the company's loyalty score is calculated at each point on the respective factor's performance scale. The second step is to calculate the range of those values for each factor. This range would be a measure of the strength of influence of the respective factor.

Unfortunately, this is often impractical. One reason is that it requires an unusually large sample size. Recognize that simply having a large total sample is not necessarily adequate; we need enough respondents at *each point* on the performance rating scale (of each factor). This has been discussed in other contexts in this chapter.

There is another aspect to this. Measuring the effect of low/high performance on a factor or attribute requires that enough respondents give low/high performance evaluations on the respective factor or attribute; the effect of high performance on "made me feel like a valued customer" cannot be determined if only a few customers give you high performance ratings on that attribute.

Interactions among Predictor Variables

As we discussed earlier, the strength of influence of attributes should not always be measured individually. One reason is interdependencies among the attributes. Another reason is the general issue of statistical interactions among the predictor variables in a driver analysis—that is, when the strength or shape of a predictor variable's influence depends on the company's performance on another predictor variable. For example, in some instances if the company performs poorly on an attribute that has a relatively strong influence, customers may become more sensitive to attributes they believe are related to that attribute, increasing their strength of influence.

ANOTHER ASPECT OF PERFORMANCE

We have been discussing company performance on attributes and factors in terms of level (for example, high and low). But quality-control practices in manufacturing have identified another aspect of quality: consistency (variation).

Consistency is important for several reasons. One is that what is called "consistency" by the company is experienced as reliability by the customer.

In the case of some attributes, a lack of reliability affects the customer's trust in the company. This is an issue because trust is a necessary condition for customer loyalty.

Another reason has to do with the necessary attributes in the penalty/reward analysis discussed earlier. The customer attrition rate can easily be as high as 50 percent among respondents giving low performance ratings on a necessary attribute. Suppose that a sizable percentage of a company's customers, say 15 percent, give the company a low rating on such an attribute. Under these conditions, without taking into account the acquisition of new customers, the company will lose 7.5 percent of its customers per year.

To determine the percentage of respondents giving a low score on an attribute, the actual distribution of responses must be examined; it cannot be inferred with very much precision from the mean score. To illustrate, two organizational units can have the same mean service score—for example, 7.5—and yet one unit has 3 percent of its scores falling in the 1–5 range while the other unit has 15 percent of its scores falling in that range. This is possible if the latter organizational unit has more high scores, which balance out the low scores.

> Under these conditions, without taking into account the acquisition of new customers, the company will lose 7.5 percent of its customers per year.

DO YOU NEED TO FIX THE SYSTEM?

As noted earlier, quality-control efforts in manufacturing have developed valuable insights into quality. Another of those insights is that variation in quality has two sources: common causes and special causes. Chakrapani (1998) describes an excellent application of this to customer service, which influenced the following discussion.

Common cause variation is variation produced by the system, broadly defined, in which employees work. Such variation can be considered "normal" for the respective system.

There are many sources of common cause variation: because of differences between stores in the number of transactions per day, the performance of the company's IT system may differ among stores; the company's employee training program may not be executed exactly as designed every time; not all supervisors are equally good; because of unavoidable human differences, no two employees perform a task in exactly the same amount of time; and the working relationship between stores and the central office may differ somewhat from store to store, because of personal relationships.

Other sources of common cause variation have to do with the larger environment. Customers differ among themselves: they vary with respect to the amount of information they need about the company's products or procedures, the complexity of their product/service requests, the ability to verbally communicate with the service person, and their expectations regarding price and service quality.

Special cause variation is produced by unusual employees or conditions—for example, extreme weather or employees who are ill.

A mathematical formula has been developed to calculate how much variation around the average level of performance is normal for the respective system—that is, due to common causes. Using a retail example, we calculate the mean service score for *each store* and then average them. Suppose this yielded a score of 38. The mathematical formula referred to is then used to calculate the amount of variation around 38 that is normal—for example, $38 - 6 = 32$ and $38 + 6 = 44$.

By definition, scores in the 32–44 range are normal for the respective system. The logical implication of this is profound: *if the company wants to move the score of any of its stores above 44, it probably must change some aspect of the system*. It is true that the manager of a particular store may find a way to overcome the system's problems and improve his or her store's score, but it is unlikely in most companies.

I know of no fact or principle that is more important in customer loyalty management than this one. Unfortunately, companies do not heed it nearly as often as they should. More often they hold accountable lower-level employees within the company, resulting in no improvement in quality.

Note that the formula for calculating the amount of normal variation should not be used if an unusual event has occurred that we would expect to influence performance, such as a new CEO or discussion in the media regarding the possible sale of the company.

EVALUATING NEW SERVICES, PROCESSES, OR TRAINING PROGRAMS

Suppose that a retailer institutes a new employee training program in some of its stores. After enough time has passed for the program to have an effect, the company conducts a customer survey and finds that, on average, the stores with the new training program have higher service evaluation scores than stores that do *not* have the new training program. With this information, can the company draw the conclusion that the new training program caused the higher service scores?

Not necessarily. For example, to ease administration of the new program the company may have introduced it in only one state, and stores in that state may have had higher service scores even *before* the new program.

Now try a different comparison. Suppose that over time the company followed the stores with the new training program and found that their service quality scores rose after the new training program began. Can the company draw the conclusion that the training program was responsible for the change? Not necessarily. For example, service quality scores may rise every year at that time because of holidays or weather. Or they may have risen at that particular time because of other changes the company made (in advertising or products) or because the competition did something that changed expectations.

There are analytical techniques available that can remove the effect of other sources of influence on customer service scores, which would allow us to draw conclusions from observed differences in service scores. But there are two obstacles to using these techniques. One is that in order to remove the effect of a given source of influence, we must be aware of that source. But in a world as complex and rapidly changing as ours, we cannot identify all the sources.

The other obstacle, frequently encountered, is a lack of data. That is, simply being aware of a given source of influence is not sufficient; we need to have information on that source (or a surrogate for that source). For example, in order to remove the effect of suburban/urban composition of a store's customers, we need to have a measure of suburban/urban for each store.

We have been talking about correctly attributing a change in service scores to the new training program, but there is another issue that should be considered: the need to generalize to all stores. That is, if the training program improved customer service scores in the stores being studied, would it do so for all stores, on average?

Going back to the earlier illustration, suppose that the new training program *did* cause the increase in the state's customer service scores. This does not necessarily mean that the training program would be effective in all states. The training program may be effective only under certain conditions, which existed in the selected state but do not exist in other states. For example, the training program may have an effect only in stores that have a large proportion of rural customers.

The problem, stated generally, is that the selected stores collectively may not be representative of all stores.

What should the company do? We can evaluate the new training program by conducting a survey research study that is designed using experimental design principles. Products (as opposed to services) have been studied in this way for several decades in many product categories. What is much less widely known is that testing of other things (for example, training programs and new services) is also possible.

A research study must be designed with a particular client situation in mind. That said, a description of a design that is appropriate in many situations follows. We will continue to use the illustration of a company that wants to know if a particular new employee training program will improve customer service. The study has the following steps:

Step 1—Draw two random samples of stores from a list of all of the company's stores. We will call one sample the treatment group and the other the control group.

Selecting stores in this manner has two benefits. One is that because of the law of averages, two samples randomly selected from the same list have a high probability of being identical to each other, except for sampling variation. The other benefit is that drawing random samples from a list of all of the company's stores enables us to generalize the results of the study to all of the company's stores.

The number of stores needed in the samples depends on the amount of store-to-store variation in service scores, the number of stores, and other issues. The greater the store-to-store variation in service scores, the more stores that are needed, although this can sometimes be mitigated by a more complex sampling plan.

Step 2—For later use, draw a random sample of customers from each store in each sample.

Step 3—Implement the employee training program in the treatment stores but not in the control stores.

Step 4—After we believe the employee training program has had sufficient time to have an effect, compare the treatment sample with the control sample with respect to their mean service quality scores. If the treatment sample's score is higher, we can reasonably conclude that this difference is probably due to the employee training program. We can draw this conclusion because, as explained earlier, the two samples were essentially identical to each other before the training program started and therefore differ only with respect to the training program.

There is a caveat, however. Store managers in the control group may hear rumors or speculation about features of the training program and modify their existing training programs to incorporate those features. This would impair our ability to draw valid conclusions from the study.

A discussion of this and alternative experimental designs can be found in Churchill (1991).

CROSS-COUNTRY COMPARISONS

Companies operating in multiple countries (or in a very heterogeneous country) often want to compare countries with respect to their responses to attitudinal rating scales. Doing this is problematic, especially when the reason involves comparing the performances of managers in different countries.

One difficulty has to do with what are commonly called cultural differences. The issue here is that a given point on a rating scale may not correspond to the same intensity of attitude in all the countries. For example, respondents who give a 9 to an overall satisfaction question in one country may not have the same level of actual overall satisfaction as respondents who give a 9 in another country. This difference may occur for many reasons; for example, one country may have cultural norms against making extreme statements.

Another difficulty, one pertaining to evaluating the performance of managers, is an *unlevel playing field*. That is, the level of product or service quality, *objectively defined*, that is necessary to achieve a given level of satisfaction may differ from one country to another. For example, the competition may be stronger in one country than in another, influencing the expectations of consumers.

We will elaborate upon these two issues separately.

Cultural Differences

Academic research and practical experience have identified several reasons that the ratings of countries may differ. Some of the more common are the following:

- Different understandings of the task of evaluating something on a linear rating scale.

- Customs regarding being polite or giving extreme responses.

- The language skills and educational level of the respondent.

- The frame of reference used by the respondent in answering the question. For example, some respondents may compare the company's performance with its performance as it is believed to be in other parts of their country, with other companies in the product category, or with companies in other product categories believed to be similar to the one under study.

- Accurately translating the meaning of the question or labels of the points on the scale from one language into another. Even subtle differences in translation can have substantial effects on responses. In some instances, the difference in translation is more than subtle. For example, in some languages there is no word or combination of words for the English word "dissatisfied"; the closest translation is "not satisfied."

- Brand image questions are especially problematic because different situations may be necessary to convey the same image and may differ in how well they do so. For example, success is characterized by different things from one country to another (amount of land owned, automobile ownership, formal educational level, family membership).

Unlevel Playing Field

The playing field is often unlevel. Some of the more common respects are as follows:

- Overall economic development of the country (transportation system, communications).

- Overall development of the product category.

- Intensity of competition within the product category.

- Attitudes about the product category. For example, beliefs about saving or borrowing money may influence responses to certain questions in financial services studies.

- The specific services or product features/benefits desired by customers may differ from one country to another, but product design decisions may not be made at the country level.

- The size of the labor pool, the experience and educational levels of its members, and their work-related beliefs and attitudes.

- Governmental restrictions on business operations.

> A difference in quality ratings between countries is not necessarily due to a difference in the amount or quality of managerial skill that has been exercised by managers in those countries.

A Partial Solution

A number of different approaches have been suggested for dealing with these issues. One of the best is described by Crosby (1992), although even it has limitations. Its strategy is to measure the degree to which culture influences responses to rating scales, and then adjust the aggregate findings of each country upward or downward accordingly to remove this effect. A slightly modified version of this approach is as follows:

Step 1—Develop a battery of rating questions covering a wide variety of nonbusiness situations. For future reference, we will call these questions the *calibration basis questions*.

Step 2—Within each country, a mean is calculated across the responses to the calibration basis questions. Let's call this the *within-country mean* for the respective country.

Step 3—An *across-country grand mean* is calculated by computing the mean of the means calculated in step 2.

Step 4—For each country separately, we calculate the difference between the two scores we have just calculated—the within-country mean and the across-country grand mean. This difference is the *culture effect*.

Step 5—The value of the culture effect is applied to the mean scores of the *customer experience questions* in each country, moving the scores upward or downward to remove the culture effect.

This approach does have limitations. The main one is that it does not address most of the unlevel playing field issues. This limitation can be removed by using an adjustment approach in which a company's scores in a given country are made relative to those of its competitors in the respective country.

WHY DID MY PERFORMANCE CHANGE?

When your score on a performance question unexpectedly changes, you naturally want to know the reason for the change. How we develop tentative explanations depends on the question.

Existing brand and advertising writings discuss possible causes for a change in brand image, so those will not be repeated here; writings that address service quality are not available, so they will be addressed.

There are certain clues that may be helpful in developing a tentative explanation for a change, as follows:

- Did the same change occur in previous years at the same time on the calendar? If so, a seasonal effect may be responsible. For example, workload may increase at certain times of the year, such as Christmas, making it difficult to maintain usual levels of service quality.

- Did the scores of all your competitors also change in the same direction? If so, the explanation has to do with the product category. For example, news stories concerning your product category may have changed customers' perceptions of all companies in the product category—for example, reports of a congressional investigation of the HMO industry.

- If the scores of some companies changed while those of others did not, try to identify respects in which those two groups of companies differ from each other, which could account for the difference in scores. For example, changes in advertising by a company may increase the importance that consumers place on a given attribute; if different brands are positioned differently with respect to that attribute, they will be affected differently.

- Did scores on some performance questions change and some not change? If so, do the questions whose scores changed have something in common? For example, if the overall evaluation of the company's performance on a factor changed, and the scores for only one of that factor's attributes changed, it is reasonable to suspect that the change in performance on that attribute caused the change in scores on the factor.

- A new marketing strategy, geographic expansion, or something else may have brought new customers into the company who differ from existing ones in terms of desired product benefits, price sensitivity, or other factors. Or it may be that, on average, new customers have higher/lower scores than other customers.

- Your customer attrition rate may have changed, thereby changing average customer tenure, and there may be a relationship between customer tenure and performance scores.

- Are there customer subpopulations or organizational units within the company whose scores changed and others whose scores did not? If so, try to identify respects in which those two groups differ from each other that could account for the difference.

- There may have been inadvertent changes in research design. Listing and explaining the different types of changes could fill several chapters: changes in the process by which the company developed a list of its customers, procedures of drawing the sample, the number of callbacks in telephone interviewing, and so on.

DETECTING CHANGES IN PERFORMANCE OVER TIME

Consider the performance of the company depicted in Figure 4.9. If these performance scores are analyzed in a pair-wise manner (January compared with August, March compared with November), there may be no two months that differ from each other, and no two multimonth periods that differ, after sampling variation is taken into account. But when we visually consider all 12 months, the scores appear to be increasing over time, albeit slowly and irregularly.

In this situation, we should use a statistical significance test that tests for a linear trend in scores over all 12 months.

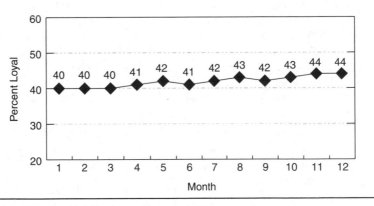

Figure 4.9 Percent loyal over time.

PERCEPTUAL MAPS

Over a period of several decades, especially in the 1970s, certain types of graphics depicting multiple brands became known as perceptual maps. Most of these maps have two axes, one vertical and one horizontal. These axes represent summarizations of the brand image attributes. That is, a statistical analysis is performed that summarizes the brand image attributes into a smaller number of new dimensions, two of which are used as axes in the map. The brands and attributes are positioned on the map in relation to these two axes (dimensions).

Several analytical techniques are alternatively used to perform the summarization: discriminate analysis, factor analysis, several versions of multidimensional scaling (MDS), and correspondence analysis (dual scaling)

Unfortunately, these maps have weaknesses that are not widely known, as follows:

- The analytical techniques differ with respect to how well they can summarize the attributes into only two dimensions. This is an issue because the map can only have two dimensions. (A page has only two dimensions, vertical and horizontal.) Additional dimensions identified during the summarization exercise are discarded.

- The "importance" of the attributes is not always shown, but when it is, it usually is not importance in the sense of strength of influence on loyalty (or some other outcome variable).

  For example, in graphics based on discriminate analysis, many users believe that the length of an arrow—each attribute is represented by an arrow—reflects the importance of the respective attribute, but this is not correct. Arrow length reflects the degree to which the brands differ in their performance ratings on the respective attribute; the fact that customers perceive the brands to differ in performance on an attribute does not necessarily indicate that that attribute is important to them.

  Correspondence analysis has the same problem. The distance of an attribute from the center (actually, the origin) of the map is often interpreted as an indication of importance, but in reality it only indicates that the brands differ in terms of their performance scores on that attribute.

- The distance between brands on the map is customarily interpreted as an indication of perceived similarity/dissimilarity of the respective brands. However, some maps are constructed such that the distance between brands on an axis is partially determined by the number of attributes summarized by the respective axis. This can be misleading because the number of attributes represented by an axis is irrelevant from a business perspective.

  For example, one of the axes may pertain to price. In most product categories only a few questions are needed to fully cover price in the questionnaire. But this does not mean that price is less important than a subject requiring a large number of questions.

- The map's two axes are not in the same unit of measure that the questionnaire used. For example, their values may range between –5 and +5. As a consequence, the practical significance of a given distance between brands on the map is unknown.

For these and other reasons, I usually recommend that other types of graphics be used. The vertical line chart, described in Chapter 3, is especially good if the number of brands is not too great (roughly speaking, not more than five).

CUSTOMER VALUE ANALYSIS

A new approach to customer loyalty management was developed in the late 1980s. The fundamental difference between it and other approaches is that it does not focus directly on loyalty, but on product value as perceived by the customer. This approach implicitly assumes that a customer's perception of a product's value influences his or her purchase behavior.

The core of this approach is a map called a customer value map, which is shown in Figure 4.10. The purpose of this map is to enable the company to determine if its prices and quality (as perceived by customers) are properly related to each other, taking the competition into account.

We will first describe how the map was constructed and interpreted when it was initially developed. We will then discuss certain drawbacks of the map and how it can be modified to address those drawbacks.

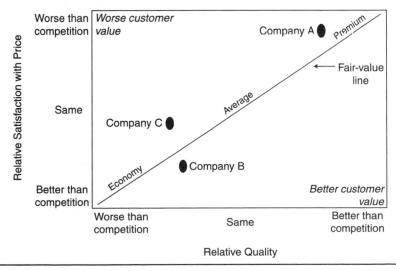

Figure 4.10   Customer value map.

Before constructing the map, you must calculate certain measures. A relative overall quality score is calculated for each company by dividing the respective company's overall quality score by the weighted average of the other companies' overall quality scores. The weights used in calculating this average are the market shares of the respective companies.

When the map was initially developed, there was not a consensus on how price should be calculated for purposes of this map. Some companies used an overall satisfaction with price question (or "offers competitive prices") to calculate relative price scores in the manner described earlier for calculating relative quality scores. Other companies used actual prices.

In the customer value map, the vertical axis is relative price, and the horizontal axis is relative quality. The companies are positioned on the map according to their scores on these two dimensions. A line, called the fair-value line, is drawn from the lower left corner of the map to the upper right corner. This line identifies the areas at which price and quality are in balance.

Companies located on the left end of the fair-value line are labeled economy brands, companies located on the right end are labeled premium brands, and companies located in the middle are labeled average.

In interpreting the map, note that the vertical axis has been flipped. That is, a position at the bottom of the map is good for the respective company and positions at the top are bad.

When this map was initially developed, most users believed that companies falling on or close to the fair-value line would almost always retain their existing market shares, assuming no major changes in the market. Companies on the right side of the page and below the fair-value line, called the better value area, were more likely to *gain* market share. Companies on the left side of the page and above the fair-value line, called the worse value area, were more likely to *lose* market share.

As originally conceived, this map has some weaknesses:

1. As stated earlier, when this map was initially developed, most users believed that companies located on or close to the fair-value line would almost always retain their existing market shares, assuming no major changes in the market. But subsequent experience and study have shown that this belief is not necessarily true. As stated earlier, companies located in the better value area of the map are more likely to gain market share. Market share that is gained by one company is necessarily taken from other companies, possibly some on the fair-value line. The chances of this happening to a company on the fair-value line are increased if it and the company in the better

value area are similar in terms of brand image, are offering similar products, or are competing in the same consumer segments.

2. By placing the fair-value line equidistant from the price and quality axes, we are saying that price and quality are equally important to consumers. This is not necessarily true, of course. The angle of the line should be adjusted to reflect the relative importance of price and quality.

3. The distance between a company and the fair-value line may not be real; that is, it may be due to sampling variability. Sampling variability can be taken into account by constructing a sampling confidence interval around the fair-value line, creating a fair-value zone.

4. As described earlier, the values used to position the companies on the map are ratios (the respective company's score divided by the average of the other companies' scores). By construction, the values of a ratio can fall between zero and positive infinity. In our situation the values have the following interpretation: a value of 1 indicates no difference between the respective company and the other companies collectively; a value between 0 and 1 indicates that the respective company is not performing as well as the other companies collectively; and a value greater than 1 indicates that the company is performing better than the competition collectively.

   Restated, values reflecting negative relationships with other companies are constrained to fall within a narrow range, 0 and 1, whereas values reflecting positive relationships are not constrained on the upper end. As a consequence, values reflecting these two relationships are not comparable. For example, a difference between 0.8 and 1 reflects a greater difference than that between 1 and 1.2, even though the absolute difference between these ratios (0.2) is the same. Consequently, the practical significance of a given distance on the value map differs from one area of the map to another—that is, from the left side to the right and from the top to the bottom. This greatly complicates interpretation of the map.

   Note that this difficulty can be avoided by using difference scores instead of ratios—that is, a company's score minus the weighted average of the other companies' scores.

5. As described earlier, a relative quality or relative price score is calculated for a given company by dividing the respective company's score by the weighted (by market share) average of the

other companies' scores. For example, the relative quality score for company A is calculated by dividing A's quality score by the weighted average of B's and C's quality scores. Therefore, a given company's relative score does not take into account the market share of that company (company A in this illustration).

6. The labels for the different areas of the fair-value line (economy, average, and premium) are probably inappropriate if the values on the relative price axis are based on price satisfaction or competitive price questions. To illustrate, it is easy to conceive of Honda and BMW owners giving the same rating to a price satisfaction question.

The practice of using these labels was probably established early in the history of customer value maps by users who used absolute price as the price (vertical) axis. In that case, these labels are appropriate.

Discussion

Intuitively, the value map makes sense when modified as described. On the other hand, few studies have been conducted that compare it to alternative approaches to managing customer loyalty. Consequently, I recommend that when the value map is used, an approach that focuses directly on loyalty also be used, and their results compared. This is one of the most fundamental rules of decision making: if you address a question using multiple approaches that differ in their assumptions and operation, and they yield the same answer, you can have more confidence in that answer than had you used only one approach to addressing the question.

Readers interested in learning more about customer value analysis can consult Kordupleski (2003).

OTHER INFLUENCES ON REPURCHASE BEHAVIOR

As explained at the beginning of the book, in order to be consistent with its usage in the industry we have used the word "loyalty" to refer to attitudinal loyalty. I would now like to make a few comments on actual repurchase behavior.

Whether a customer continues to purchase your products depends not only on attitudinal loyalty, but on certain conditions within, or characteristics of, the product/service category. Some of the more important ones are as follows:

- Purchase convenience of product currently used

- Availability and convenience of competing products

- Amount of effort and resources required to decide which product to switch to

- Cost and amount of effort required to leave current company

- Cost and amount of effort required to join new company

- Perceived risk that is incurred with switching

- Importance of the product category to customers

- Product visibility and advertising at point of sale

- Habit/inertia

- Variety-seeking purchase behavior

- How effectively products in other categories can be used instead

A few words of elaboration on the subject of risk: risk is a function of (1) seriousness of the functional and emotional consequences of a "wrong" choice, (2) perceived likelihood of a choice being wrong, and (3) perceived ease of obtaining recompense if a wrong choice is made. It is in this context that we hear the remark, "The devil you know is better than the one you don't know." That is, a customer who is dissatisfied with his or her current product/service may be uncertain about the quality of competing products and doesn't want to find out the hard way that their quality is even worse.

Recognize that these conditions and characteristics strongly influence the maximum level of repurchase behavior at the individual customer level that is practically possible in your product category. Of course, these conditions and characteristics may change over time and should be monitored.

Some of these conditions and characteristics also influence how great an advantage in value a competitor must attain in order to lure customers away from you. To illustrate, suppose that a customer is dissatisfied with your product. If the stores in that customer's usual shopping area offer only your product and the nearest store that offers a competitor's product is two miles away, the customer will probably go to the closer store (and buy your product) if the two products are perceived to differ in quality by only half a point on a 10-point scale. But if the competing product is perceived to be 5 points better, the customer will probably drive the extra miles to buy it.

This is a simplified illustration, of course, as it does not take into account the importance of the product category to the customer.

Note that even if the person had never before used the competing product, he or she could probably compare it to your product. How is this possible? By brand image. That is, the consumer projects his or her perceptions of the brand onto its products.

> These conditions and characteristics strongly influence the maximum level of repurchase behavior that is practically possible in your product/service category.
>
> They also influence how great an advantage in value a competitor must attain in order to lure customers away from you.

Bibliography

Aaker, D. A. 1991. *Managing Brand Equity.* New York: The Free Press.

———. 1996. *Building Strong Brands.* New York: The Free Press.

Barlow, J., and D. Maul. 2000. *Emotional Value: Creating Strong Bonds with Your Customers.* San Francisco: Berrett-Koehler Publishers.

Barsky, J., and L. Nash. 2003. "Customer Satisfaction: Applying Concepts to Industrywide Measures." *Cornell Hotel and Restaurant Administration Quarterly* 44 (5–6): 177.

Carbone, L. P. 2004. *Clued In: How to Keep Customers Coming Back Again and Again.* Upper Saddle River, NJ: Financial Times Prentice Hall.

Chakrapani, C. 1998. *How to Measure Service Quality & Customer Satisfaction.* Chicago: American Marketing Association.

Churchill, G. Jr. 1991. *Marketing Research: Methodological Foundations.* 5th ed. Chicago: Dryden Press.

Crosby, L. 1992. "Toward a Common Verbal Scale of Perceived Quality." In *The Race Against Expectations.* Amsterdam: European Society for Opinion and Marketing Research.

Dutka, A. 1995. *AMA Handbook for Customer Satisfaction.* Lincolnwood, IL: NTC Business Books.

Edwardson, M. 1998. "Measuring Consumer Emotions in Service Encounters: An Exploratory Analysis." *Australasian Journal of Market Research* 6 (2): 10, 13.

Freund, R., R. Littell, and P. Spector. 1986. *SAS System for Linear Models.* Cary, NC: SAS Institute.

Garvin, D. 1988. *Managing Quality: The Strategic and Competitive Edge.* New York: The Free Press.

Gilmore, J., and B. Pine II. 2002. *The Experience IS the Marketing.* Louisville, KY: BrownHerron.

Keller, K. 1998. *Strategic Brand Management.* Upper Saddle River, NJ: Prentice Hall.

Kim, J. J. 2006. "A Latte with Your Loan?" *Wall Street Journal,* May 17, p. D1.

Koratpleski, R. 2003. *Mastering Customer Value Management.* Cincinnati, OH: Pinnaflex Educational Resources.

Naumann, E., and K. Giel. 1995. *Customer Satisfaction Measurement and Management.* Milwaukee, WI: ASQC Quality Press.

Pine, B. II, and J. Gilmore. 1999. *The Experience Economy: Work Is Theatre and Every Business a Stage.* Boston: Harvard Business School Press.

Reichheld, F. 2006. *The Ultimate Question: Driving Good Profits and True Growth.* Boston: Harvard Business School Press.

Richins, M. L. 1997. "Measuring Emotions in the Consumption Experience." *Journal of Consumer Research* 24 (September): 144–45.

Schmitt, B. H. 1999. *Experiential Marketing: How to Get Customers to Sense, Feel, Think, Act, Relate.* New York: The Free Press.

———. 2003. *Customer Experience Management: A Revolutionary Approach to Connecting with Your Customers.* Hoboken, NJ: John Wiley & Sons.

Schneider, B., and D. Bowen. 1999. "Understanding Customer Delight and Outrage." *Sloan Management Review* 40 (Fall): 35–45.

Shaw, C., and J. Ivens. 2002. *Building Great Customer Experiences.* New York: Palgrave Macmillan.

Sheth, J., B. Mittal, and B. Newman. 1999. *Customer Behavior: Consumer Behavior and Beyond.* Fort Worth, TX: Harcourt Brace College Publishers.

Smith, E. R. 2000. *e-Loyalty: How to Keep Customers Coming Back to Your Website.* New York: HarperCollins Publishers.

Smith, S., and J. Wheeler. 2002. *Managing the Customer Experience: Turning Customers into Advocates.* London: Financial Times Prentice Hall.

Underhill, P. 1999. *Why We Buy: The Science of Shopping.* New York: Simon & Schuster.

Zeithaml, V., A. Parasuraman, and L. Berry. 1990. *Delivering Quality Service: Balancing Customer Perceptions and Expectations.* New York: The Free Press.

Index